ATHENS, ROME, AND ENGLAND

ATHENS, ROME, AND ENGLAND

AMERICA'S CONSTITUTIONAL HERITAGE

MATTHEW A. PAULEY

GRIFFON HOUSE PUBLICATIONS

In memory of my dear mother

Library of Congress Cataloging-in-Publication Data

Pauley, Matthew A., 1959– author.
  Athens, Rome, and England : America's constitutional heritage / Matthew A. Pauley.
    pages cm
Summary: "Traces the development of constitutional law and theory from classical time through medieval England up to the time of the drafting of the US Constitution, demonstrating a through line of development"—Provided by publisher.
  ISBN 978-1-61017-083-3 (paperback)
  1. Constitutional history—United States. 2. Constitutional history—England. 3. Roman law—History. 4. Law, Greek—History. I. Title.
  KF4541.P39 2014
  342.7302'4—dc23
                          2013050738

Published in the United States by

Griffon House Publications
in association with
Intercollegiate Studies Institute
3901 Centerville Road
Wilmington, Delaware 19807-1938
www.isibooks.org

Manufactured in the United States of America

Contents

ATHENS, ROME, AND ENGLAND

PREFACE

The idea for this book occurred to me as I was teaching seminars in constitutional law and history at Manhattanville College in Purchase, New York. Many of the best students both at Manhattanville and across the United States are interested in contemporary American law in general and the American Constitution in particular. Too few of them, however, have a strong knowledge of the ancient and English historical background of American law. To help provide students with some of that background, I began teaching what I called perspective seminars and writing brief chapters on the constitutional histories of ancient Athens and Rome and of England to supplement the readings in these seminars.

There are, of course, many excellent histories of Athens, Rome, and England. Not many, however, provide college and law students with a readable survey in a short volume that highlights those parts of the constitutional development that are of interest and relevance to the American experience. I have tried to provide such a survey, a narrative sketch of the constitutional development of those three regimes, with emphasis on those moments that illuminate and are illuminated by the American constitutional experience. This book is designed for anyone curious about the evolution of constitutions in the past as well as about the historical foundations and antecedents of America's legal and political institutions.

It is divided into three parts. After an introduction that sets forth some of the main features of America's constitutional system, Part One turns to the constitution of ancient Athens, highlighting some similarities and differences between the ancient Greek constitutional experience and our own before proceeding, chronologically, with a survey of ancient Athenian constitutional history, from Draco's and Solon's early aristocratic constitutions, through the democratic revolution and the golden age, to the age of Plato and Aristotle and the decline of the polis. Part Two does much the same for Rome, beginning with a survey of some of Rome's most important contributions to our constitutional system and moving on to a study of ancient Roman constitutional history, from the monarchy to the Republic and beyond to the Empire.

Part Three, "The English Constitution and English Common Law," is by far the longest section because there is so much in the history of England's constitution before the colonization of America that is of tremendous relevance to our form of government and law. It opens with a brief introduction to some key aspects of the English legacy for American law, followed by several chapters, each subdivided to carry the reader easily through the many important stages in the development of the English constitution—from the Roman and Anglo-Saxon constitutions through the Middle Ages and the Tudor and Stuart eras. The Conclusion highlights the American constitutional experience, emphasizing the influence of the classical and common law background on our legal system.

I am deeply indebted to the late Dr. Anne Paolucci, who read the manuscript with care, as well as to my colleagues and students at Manhattanville College for their inspiration.

Matthew A. Pauley
October 2013

INTRODUCTION

Alexis de Tocqueville once said that, in America, every political or policy issue tends, sooner or later, to become a constitutional issue. Today the Constitution influences nearly every aspect of our lives. There are, of course, profound disagreements about what the Constitution means and how it should be interpreted. For all their differences, however, liberals and conservatives both agree that the Constitution is America's sacred text, our cherished fundamental law.

It is often said that America is unique in having the oldest constitution in the world. Certainly other nations have written constitutions, but they are not as old as ours. Other nations have had constitutional law dating back earlier than America's, as well as a series of documents that together can be labeled a constitution. Ancient Athens, for example, had Draco's code of laws and Solon's constitution. Ancient Rome had the Twelve Tables and Justinian's *Corpus Juris*. England has had Magna Carta, the Petition of Right, and a Bill of Rights, among many other documents. Still, it is said, no nation has had one written constitution for as long as America has.

In a certain sense, this is true. It is a reason for national pride, and justifiably so. Saying that our Constitution is oldest, however, presupposes a particular modern and American definition of what a constitution is. It assumes that a constitution is a written text—a single document of fundamental law.

This is not what most people in the past have understood a constitution to be. Through most of history, a constitution has been understood to refer to a country's form of government and law. This would include not only the type of government—what the ancients would call government of one, few, or many, for example—but also the whole legal and governmental system, the court structure, and so on. As Aristotle wrote, the form of "the community is the constitution."

Viewed from this perspective, America's Constitution is far more than the single document of that title. It includes our whole system of representative democracy, our court structure, our traditions of civil and criminal, public and private, law. It includes also basic ideas about representation, freedom, and equality, which are central to our constitutional experience.

Perhaps the one idea most central to the American Constitution is respect for the rule of law. This principle explains key clauses in the text of the Constitution, including the prohibition on bills of attainder and ex post facto laws. More important, it informs the whole spirit of our law—and that fact has not been forgotten by the justices who have interpreted our Constitution over the years. In his dissenting opinion in *Morrison v. Olson* in 1988, Justice Scalia said that it "is the proud boast of our democracy that we have 'a government of laws and not of men.'"[1] Echoing the English jurist Bracton, who wrote in about AD 1200 that the king was "not under man but under God and the Law," Supreme Court justice Robert Jackson stressed the accountability of the president under the law in his concurring opinion in *Youngstown Sheet and Tube Co. v. Sawyer*, invalidating President Truman's seizure of the steel mills in the Korean War: "The essence of free government is "learn to live…underneath the law."… With all its defects, delays, and inconveniences, men have discovered no technique for long preserving free government except that the Executive be under the law, and that the law be made by parliamentary deliberations."[2]

Beyond the rule of law, individual rights are, of course, another central element of the American Constitution. The whole of our legal discourse is dominated today by what Mary Ann Glendon of Harvard

University has aptly called "rights talk." Those rights are protected by a tradition of common law and by judges armed with judicial review, the power to declare acts of legislatures to be unconstitutional and therefore void.

In short, any summary of the American Constitution would have to point to our emphasis on the rule of law, individual rights, our common law tradition, and our tradition of a written Constitution enforced by judicial review. It would also have to include the fact that ours is not a pure democracy, but rather a republican government.

James Madison spoke in *The Federalist Papers* of two auxiliary precautions to ensure the preservation of liberty. The first, of course, was separation of powers and checks and balances. The second was federalism and representation, and it is Madison himself who explains, in *Federalist* No. 10, why the anti-Federalists were wrong to assert that free government is only possible on a small scale. On the contrary, Madison says, extend the sphere in a larger republic of representatives from many states, and liberty flourishes as the danger from majority faction recedes.

To call our Constitution republican, however, is not to deny that it was intended to have and does have very real democratic features. In his book *America's Constitution: A Biography*, Yale law professor Akhil Reed Amar emphasizes this democratic theme. Amar begins by noting that the words of the Preamble—"We the People...do ordain and establish this Constitution"—"did more than promise popular self government. They also embodied and enacted it." Just as the words "I do" formalize a wedding ceremony and the words "I accept" complete a contract, these words of the Preamble are "not merely a text but a deed—a constituting. We the People do ordain. In the late 1780s, this was the most democratic deed the world had ever seen."[3]

Amar reminds us that, although there was no popular referendum on the Constitution, the ratifying conventions in each of the states did represent "the people" more directly than the ordinary state legislatures. Perhaps inspired by the opening words of the Preamble, many states "waived standard voting restrictions and allowed a uniquely

broad class of citizens to vote for ratification convention delegates."
Amar gives the example of New York, which "temporarily set aside
its usual property qualifications and, for the first time in its history,
invited all free adult male citizens to vote." Other states did much the
same, allowing a remarkably wide proportion of the free population to
vote for the convention delegates. Amar summarizes the democratic
implications: "All told, eight states elected convention delegates under
special rules that were more populist and less property focused than
normal, and two others followed standing rules that let virtually all
taxpaying adult male citizens vote. No state employed special election
rules that were more property based or less populist than normal."[4]

For their part, the Founding Fathers emphasized the democratic
character of what they were doing. James Wilson, America's most
prominent lawyer and only one of six people who had signed both
the Constitution and the Declaration of Independence, emphasized
the importance of popular ratification: "This Constitution...is laid
before the citizens of the United States, unfettered by restraint....By
their fiat, it will become of value and authority; without it, it will
never receive the character of authenticity and power."[5]

The Constitution text itself had democratic features. We have
become so accustomed to modern versions of Charles Beard's "Economic Interpretation of the Constitution," that we have forgotten that
the words "private property" do not appear in the Preamble or anywhere in the original document.

Words like "the people" and "republican," of course, do. Article
I boldly proclaims that the House of Representatives is to be elected
directly by the people. Neither the states nor the federal government
may grant titles of nobility. Government employees are to be paid a
salary out of the public treasury to ensure that wealthy aristocrats are
not the only ones to take office. Article VI provides that juries of ordinary citizens will counterbalance the role of judges in criminal trials.
Article IV guarantees every state in the union a republican form of
government.

For all its democratic character, however, it is undeniably true that we can call the American Constitution of 1787—and the process of its ratification—democratic only if we add "democratic by the standards of the time." No women voted for the Constitution, or participated in the Constitutional Convention or in any of the ratification debates. Slaves, of course, played no role. Neither did white males without property.

America, in other words, did not begin as any sort of democracy. Rather, there was a gradual democratization of America—a process that proceeded by slow stages from what Aristotle and Polybius among the Greek philosophers called government of one, to government of few, to government of many.

This brings us to a vitally important point. When the American Constitution is viewed broadly to mean our whole form of government and law, it could be said that we have not had only one constitution throughout our history. Rather we have had a series of constitutions—a series of types of government, each significantly different from the one before. In the beginning, America was ruled by one—the king of England. Then came the rule of few—the aristocracy of the Founding Fathers, who, for all their democratic "talk," conducted their Constitutional Convention in complete secrecy with sentries posted at the doors to prevent any member of the "public" from getting in or learning anything of what was taking place.

The first stage of democratization of the American Constitution came in the Jacksonian era in the 1830s. For the first time, presidential candidates were selected by conventions rather than by closed "congressional caucus." Movements to abolish property qualifications for voting accelerated. Some of the new states admitted to the union adopted universal white manhood suffrage. Many state offices, especially judgeships, became elective. By the year Andrew Jackson became president, in 1829, all but two of the nation's twenty-four states had selected presidential electors by popular ballot rather than by a vote of the state legislature. Jackson's Democratic Party was the forerunner of the mass-based political party of today. As one constitutional historian notes, it "aimed not merely to nominate candidates and coordinate efforts of like-minded persons in the government, but to recruit rank-and-file supporters, retain their loyalty, and, by winning elections, supposedly give voice to the will of the people."[6]

Later, of course, came the Civil War amendments, which widened the suffrage to include freed slaves and, for the first time, gave American citizens rights against their own states. In the later nineteenth and early twentieth centuries, the Progressive movement produced a series of constitutional democratic reforms—from the Seventeenth Amendment providing for direct popular election of senators to the Nineteenth Amendment guaranteeing women the right to vote. In the later part of the twentieth century, America's Constitution was democratized further still, with the abolition of the poll tax and the extension of the franchise to those aged eighteen to twenty-one, as well as with the passage of a series of revolutionary civil rights acts in the 1960s, guaranteeing equal rights under the law.

In the last analysis, then, America's Constitution must be seen as far more than one text, even a text that has been amended over the years. It contains our whole system of government and law, and that system has evolved slowly but significantly over the course of our more than two hundred years as a nation.

The details of that evolution, though interesting in themselves, are, for the most part, the subject of another book. Any sophisticated student of his own nation's law, however, is also interested in the law of other countries.

America is not the only country in history with a constitution in this broad sense. Countless nations, of course, have had a variety of forms of government and law. Some have even had many of the features of our type of constitution, with limited government, checks and balances, separation of powers, and a representative republican tradition.

Of all past civilizations that have had constitutions, three stand out as being particularly worthy of our attention—ancient Athens, ancient Rome, and England. For one thing, all three of these constitutions had some basic points of similarity with our Constitution.

Athens, for example, like us, had an emphasis on the rule of law and, at least for a time, a kind of democracy. Rome, like us, had a profound sense of law as a science, with libraries and scholars of law. England, like us, has had representative government and the tradition of the common law. Second, all three profoundly influenced the American Constitution. From Athens, for instance, we inherited the humanist orientation of our law. From Rome, among much else, we got our commitment to natural law. From England, we got the jury system, writs like habeas corpus, and stare decisis or precedent.

Each of these three constitutions can be said to be imperfect examples of or experiments in what can be called, for want of a better term, constitutionalism.

In his still-authoritative treatise *Constitutionalism: Ancient and Modern*, Harvard professor Charles Howard McIlwain offered a definition, borrowed from Thomas Paine's *Rights of Man*:

> That there is a fundamental difference between a people's government and that people's constitution, whether the government happens to be entrusted to a king or to a representative assembly. That this constitution is "antecedent" to the government. That it defines the authority which the people commits to its government, and in so doing thereby limits it. That any exercise of authority beyond these limits by any government is an exercise of "power without right."[7]

America has continued that experiment in constitutionalism, but it would be wrong to presume that we have a monopoly on it. Other countries have tried it. In today's world, it might with candor be said that one way of distinguishing nations friendly to our interests from those not friendly is by asking whether the government adheres to a tradition of constitutionalism. In other words, is it limited by fundamental law or is it some kind of dictatorship?

Aristotle taught us more than two thousand years ago that good constitutions are those that look to the common good while constitutions that seek to promote only the good of the rulers are perverted or bad. This observation takes on renewed importance in today's world of terrorism. It had a similar urgency when McIlwain lectured on the subject at Cornell in 1938–39 on the eve of World War II. McIlwain explains, in words that seem appropriate for us today:

> The time seems to be propitious for an examination of the general principle of constitutionalism—our own Anglo-Saxon brand of it in particular—and an examination which should include some consideration of the successive stages in its development. For perhaps never in its long history has the principle of constitutionalism been so questioned as it is questioned today, never has the attack upon it been so determined or so threatening as it is just now. The world is trembling in the balance between the orderly procedure of law and the processes of force which seem so much more quick and effective. We must make our choice between these two. . . . If we are to make that choice intelligently, it would seem reasonable . . . that we should retrace the history of our constitutionalism . . . to estimate its past achievements.[8]

McIlwain knew even in 1939 that there was no more important time to study constitutionalism. With the free world now immersed in another type of world war against terrorists, the importance of that study once again becomes evident.

There is no better way to study the history of constitutionalism than to study the evolution of the ancient Athenian, Roman, and English constitutions—all three in some measure and in varying degrees, experiments that left their mark. There is, however, still one more important reason for this study. Each of these constitutions, like ours, evolved. Each grew and changed dramatically over the course of years as social, political, and international conditions altered. Some of those changes brought those constitutions more in line with things recognizable to us. Other changes led those constitutions in directions far different from those in which we have ever gone or perhaps ever plan or care to go. The story of how each of those constitutions developed over centuries is a fascinating and compelling one. No student of law and government can afford to ignore it.

This book traces the historical evolution of those three constitutions—their laws and government—with emphasis on those elements that shed light on the American constitutional experience. In some places, parallels with us are close; in others, differences loom large; in still other places, those constitutions are far removed from ours.

Cicero once said that to be ignorant of what has taken place in former times is to continue always a child. This book is meant to provide a deeper understanding of the three great constitutions that helped form us and that have left their indelible mark on the rest of the world as well.

PART ONE

The Constitution of Ancient Athens

ONE

Ancient Greece and American Constitutionalism

In their humanism and in their preference for the rule of law, the ancient Greeks were remarkably similar to us and greatly influenced our constitutional tradition. On the other hand, they differed sharply from us in their attitude toward international relations and in the kind of union and level of participation in democratic government they favored. In this respect, they gave our Founding Fathers an example of what they did not want to do. A study of the democratic constitutional development of ancient Athens can do much to show the relevance of the Greek experience to American constitutionalism.

The first three words of the American Constitution—*We the People*—are unquestionably the most famous and, in some ways, the most significant in our recorded history. Unlike the Codes of Hammurabi and Lipit-Ishtar in ancient times, our fundamental law does not begin with an invocation of the gods and the divine origins of the state. The father of our Constitution, James Madison, was acutely aware, as he puts it in *The Federalist Papers*, that men are not angels and that angels are not to govern men. The public order for us is made by humans, for humans.

America's greatest chief justice, John Marshall, recognized this fact in his famous opinion for the Supreme Court in the 1819 case of *McCulloch v. Maryland*. Rejecting Maryland's argument that the states retained their sovereignty after entering the union, Marshall reminded his contemporaries that the Constitution had been ratified, not by the state legislatures, but by conventions chosen in each state by the people. In all respects, Marshall went on, the constitutional system draws power from the people: "The government of the Union, then,... is emphatically and truly a government of the people. In form, and in substance, it emanates from them. Its powers are granted by them, and are to be exercised directly on them, and for their benefit."[1]

This humanism of American law has its roots in ancient Greece. The Greeks were the world's first humanists. Theirs was, of course, not the world's first great civilization. The Egyptians, for example, gave the world fantastic architecture, among much else. From our humanistic point of view today, however, Egyptian art and literature appear superstitious and stultifying. The Sphinx with its lion's body and man's head seems a perfect symbol of their fantastic conceptions of gods who were not human but rather monstrous combinations of animals. Egyptian religious and legal customs seemed primitive to the ancient Greeks who later documented them. One example is recorded by the Greek historian Herodotus on his visit to Egypt: "When a cat dies in a house, its inmates shave their eyebrows; When a dog dies, they shave body and head all over."[2]

By contrast, Greek gods were designed as "big men"—with human virtues and vices. Moreover, in art, in religion, in philosophy, and especially in politics and law, the focus of the ancient Greeks was on everything pertaining to the welfare and fortunes of man in this world. As one historian puts it, it is hard to imagine "the 'wily Odysseus' obeying an order to shave his eyebrows because a cat had died or to fasten golden bracelets on the front paws of a sacred crocodile."[3]

That was a new way of looking at the world then, and it is still with us now. We are reminded of it every time we consider what Abraham Lincoln meant when he spoke at Gettysburg of "government of the people, by the people, for the people."

As Lincoln also understood well, America's international relations begins with the Declaration of Independence. In the penultimate sentence of that document, Thomas Jefferson made clear the prerogatives of "the separate and equal station" that he was claiming for the new nation. The basic principle of our foreign policy is to be a nation and respect the right of other sovereign nations to a "separate and equal station" among the powers of the earth.

The Greeks of antiquity had a different approach to international relations. Like the ancient Hebrews, who called all non-Hebrews Gentiles ("other people"), they knew that they were different from all other people in the world. They divided the world into two groups—the Hellenes (which they called themselves, for the ancient Greeks never used the Roman word *Greek* to describe themselves) and the barbarians.

The term *Hellene* was used to signify the common tie of kinship shared by all the different clans, ethnic groups, and cities of the area known now as Greece, as well as its colonies. Everyone beyond "Hellas" was considered "barbarian." But the ancient Greeks did not mean barbarian in the modern sense—not someone who ate raw meat or lived in a cave. The word *barbarian* for them did not carry the same pejorative connotations that it does for us. It only meant people who made a noise like "bar bar" instead of speaking Greek. The Greeks respected other peoples. They even envied some of them sometimes. But they were always conscious of being different from them.

If asked why he was different from barbarians, an ancient Greek would probably say,, "Those peoples are all slaves. We Hellenes are free men." To anyone acquainted with ancient Greek history, this may seem an exaggeration. Even during the classical age, not all Greeks lived in a democracy. Not all ruled themselves. Nevertheless, they believed strongly in the rule of law, that state business was public business and not the private concern of the ruler. They were hostile to arbitrary rule. They had kings—Sparta, for example, was never a democracy—but in their very souls the idea of an absolute arbitrary monarch was alien to them.

A story from the great Greek historian of the Persian Wars, Herodotus, can help illustrate this. Herodotus tells of how a great Persian king was caught in a storm at sea. When his skipper advised him to lighten the ship, the king ordered his courtiers to jump overboard.

Later, on reaching land in safety, he first decorated his skipper for his wisdom, then beheaded him for the crime of causing the death of his courtiers. Herodotus repeats this story as an example of loathsome tyranny. The lesson is not lost on modern ears. As one contemporary historian puts it, "whoever was armed with executive power should always be ... answerable for its use, and a Persian king was answerable to no one."[4]

In his introduction to *Originalism: A Quarter-Century of Debate*, a book celebrating the twenty-fifth anniversary of the Federalist Society, Professor Steven Calabresi of Northwestern University Law School reminds us how deeply committed America also is to the rule of law. "We believe," he writes, "that ours should be a government of laws and not one of men or of judges." A jurisprudence of "originalism" that relies on the intent of the framers in constitutional interpretation is, in Calabresi's view, the best way to remain faithful to this commitment.

The emphasis on the rule of law is central to originalism. Originalists believe that the written constitution is our fundamental law and that it binds all of us—even Supreme Court justices. Those justices who abandon the original meaning of the text of the Constitution inevitably end up substituting their own political philosophies for those of the framers. We Americans have to decide whether we want a government of laws or one of judges.[5]

Attorney General Ed Meese made much the same point in his now famous 1985 speech to the American Bar Association, which is credited, by Calabresi among others, with having introduced the jurisprudence of originalism "into noisy and public view." Quoting Tom Paine, Meese said that we "Americans ... rightly pride ourselves on having produced the greatest political wonder of the world—a government of laws and not of men. Thomas Paine was right: 'America has no monarch. Here the law is king.'"[6]

Like the ancient Greeks, we advocate the rule of law, and like them we despise arbitrary government. In this age of terror, that is principally how we distinguish our form of government from that of our enemies. We implicitly recognize the truth of the observation of Aristotle, who summed up the political experience of the Greeks for us when he said that good constitutions are those in which the rulers act in the interest of the people while perverted constitutions are those in which the rulers act only for themselves.

Our Founding Fathers were, of course, acutely aware of the danger that the rulers would, even in a representative democracy, act in their own interest and not for the good of the whole. This concern is what motivates James Madison, in *Federalist* No. 10, to argue about the dangers of majority factions—groups of people with an interest adverse to the rights of other citizens or to the common good of the society as a whole. Madison's solution is to control the effects of factions by widening the sphere—enlarging the size of the union so as to make it more difficult for majority factions to form and carry out their schemes of oppression.

By contrast to us, however, the ancient Greeks remained divided and never, at least in the classical period, achieved what our Constitution calls a "more perfect Union" of the Greek people. In ancient times, the mountains and the water divided the Greeks into many different states—each independent of the other. Each guarded its independence fiercely. At times they allied with one another, but on the whole, each retained its independence.

There is nothing in our experience of modern states comparable to the Greek city-states. The total area of the mainland of ancient Hellas was less than that of the state of Maine. And that small area was divided into fiercely independent city-states.

Historian Herbert Newell Couch of Brown University reminds us to keep a proper perspective when studying ancient Greece: "It is important to modify the inevitable modern concept of large political units like the United States and to picture clearly the miniature geographic scale on which the drama of politics, war, trade, and alliance was played in the ancient world."[7]

It would, of course, be impossible to understand what it means to say that the United States is the most powerful nation in the world without knowing what is meant by the term nation. The great German philosopher G. W. F. Hegel taught us that the West has, in modern times, produced "a world not of vast despotic states including many nations, and not of single nations divided into many little states. These two opposed principles of antiquity, both based on slavery, are reconciled in the modern world's ideal of the nation state."[8]

Similarly, to understand politics in antiquity, and in ancient Greece in particular, one has to come to terms with what the polis signified. British classicist H. D. F. Kitto insists on this basic premise: "Without a clear conception of what the polis was, and what it meant to the Greeks, it is quite impossible to understand properly Greek history, the Greek mind, or Greek achievement."[9]

In his *Republic*, Plato would later posit a limit of five thousand citizens for his ideal state. Aristotle in his *Politics* says that each citizen should be able to recognize every other citizen in the polis by sight. We cannot imagine living in a state that is so small that one could walk across it in one day. But we must not confuse small size with triviality. Kitto explains this in a brilliant passage where he tells how to assess the Greek city-state properly in order to grasp its significance:

> To think on this scale is difficult for us, who regard a state of ten million as small, and are accustomed to states which, like the U.S.A. and the U.S.S.R., are so big that they have to be referred to by their initials; but when the adjustable reader has become accustomed to the scale, he will not commit the vulgar error of confusing size with significance. The modern writer is sometimes heard to speak with splendid scorn of "those petty Greek states, with their interminable quarrels." Quite so, [they]...are petty, compared with modern size. The Earth itself is petty, compared with Jupiter—but then, the atmosphere of Jupiter is mainly ammonia, and that makes a difference. We do not like breathing ammonia, and the Greeks would not much have liked breathing the atmosphere of the vast modern State. They knew

of one such, the Persian Empire, and thought it very suitable, for barbarians.[10]

Above all, the ancient Greek polis was a community, and a community in which the affairs of the whole polis were truly the affairs of every citizen. This is the meaning behind Socrates's analogy, in Plato's *Republic*, to a person cutting his finger: the whole body feels the pain of the part. This is why Aristotle says in his *Politics* that citizenship does not depend on residence but on active participation in the affairs of the city. This is also what Thucydides means in his *History*, where he recounts Pericles saying in his Funeral Oration that "a man who does not take part in public affairs is good for nothing."[11] The ancient Greeks had a term for such persons—*idiotes*, from which we, of course, derive our word *idiot*.

In modern-day London, the monument to Admiral Lord Nelson in Trafalgar Square is inscribed with the famous words Nelson is said to have uttered at the great naval battle in which he gave his life for England's victory against the navy of Napoleon: "England expects every man to do his duty." President John F. Kennedy echoed this sentiment in his Inaugural Address when he urged his fellow Americans to "ask not what your country can do for you, ask what you can do for your country." The ancient Greeks would surely have understood such an idea, although they might have wondered why people had to be reminded of it.

In postclassical Greece, the orator Demonsthenes will later speak with contempt of the man who "avoids the polis." And Aristotle will say of the man "who is without a city-state" that he is "either a poor specimen or else superhuman." Indeed, Aristotle quotes Homer to describe such a man without a country: "clanless, lawless, and hearthless is he."[12]

This sense of community in the ancient Greek polis bears emphasis precisely because it is so different from our modern, especially American conception. In our search for parallels, we often forget that, in many ways, the Greek experience is alien to ours. As Robert Morkot reminds us in the *Penguin Historical Atlas of Ancient Greece*, "the Greeks were probably more unlike us than we have ever allowed."[13]

One respect in which they were unlike us is surely their strong sense of political community. For an American in the twenty-first century, the "state" is often that entity which takes our money in the form of taxes. We do not relish paying taxes anymore than we take pleasure in serving on juries, or voting, or registering for the draft. These are all activities the state imposes on us. Even in the aftermath of the national tragedy of 9/11, many Americans take for granted the privileges our democracy offers but seem reluctant to sacrifice for the public good as a worthy goal.

It was considered a worthy goal in ancient Greece, particularly ancient Athens. With this contrast in mind, a comparison of the stages of the democratic constitutional and political development of ancient Athens with our own democratic development can shed a powerful light on our American constitutional heritage.

Two

The Evolution of Athenian Democracy:
Model and Contrast for American Democratic
Development

We have seen how much of the humanism of American law is derived from the experience of the ancient Greeks. American law in general and the American Constitution in particular are more than just humanist or "people-oriented," however. As we have seen, they are also fundamentally democratic in character. Near the end of the Introduction, we briefly reviewed how America's democracy evolved and broadened. Ancient Greece in general and Athens in particular went through a comparable democratic development—from government of one to government of few to government of many. A survey of the democratic development of this ancient civilization can thus greatly illuminate America's democratic experiment.

The Athenians, like their fellow Greeks and like the American colonies, started with a rule of one. Athens in its infancy—before around 600 BC—was ruled by a king, the head of the tribe, who, like our chief executive, was commander in chief at wartime. Under the king were several chieftains who formed a council—something like our Senate or Supreme Court—to advise the king. The common people were assembled, on occasion, in what the medieval English would later call a "moot," a remote ancestor of our House of Representatives, to give assent to the council's advice by banging their shields or to express their disapproval by booing.[1]

One can get a good picture of this early Greek type of constitution by reading Homer's description of Agamemnon as a "king of Greek kings." Such a king does not rule absolutely, as political scientist Richard Neustadt reminds us in describing our presidents, who must persuade others around them to get their way. Agamemnon must persuade the elders, a sort of aristocracy of the oldest and best warriors, as well as an assembly of the rank and file of the army, to get what he wants.

Unlike an American president, however, Agamemnon's authority is derived not from the people below but from the gods above. He is a "Zeus spawned king," not a popular magistrate elected by the people, albeit indirectly through an Electoral College. He is a leader who talks with the gods in his dreams and passes on what he has heard. Delivering a kind of State of the Union Address to his assembled troops, King Agamemnon tests them by urging them to give up the battle and flee for home. Thersites, one of the rank-and-file soldiers, challenges Agamemnon, claiming that it's "not right for a leader to march our troops into battle."[2]

Such a speech might be drawn from the editorial pages of some of today's newspapers. In Homer, of course, the speaker is ridiculed as a "blathering fool and a rabble rouser," and when Odysseus "whaled the staff down on Thersites' back," we are invited to consider this as a just punishment for his unpatriotic and treasonous remarks.

In this respect, the *Iliad* is a glorification of the heroism of the aristocratic noble class over the ignorance of the common man. Just as the British monarchy of one gave way to the aristocracy of our Founding Fathers, in archaic Greece these nobles played an increasingly important role in the life of the city. Only the nobles could wear bronze armor and ride on horses. Law was revealed to the nobles. They did not make law; they discovered it. They were the best people— *aristoi*—who had access to the law. By the eighth and seventh centuries BC, in Athens and elsewhere in ancient Greece, the kings were losing their power to these cavalry-riding nobles.

By 700 BC, Athens had moved from a monarchy to an aristocracy— a change that parallels the transformation of America from the rule of George III to that of the Founding Fathers. The king's functions were parceled out among a Board of Nine Archons, which was selected by the nobles, now in control of Athens.

In our case, the aristocracy of our Founding Fathers created a Constitution that could be adapted to the social and economic changes of American society. The introduction of steamboat navigation and the rise of the railroads, for example, influenced the Supreme Court's changing interpretation of the commerce and contracts clauses in cases like *Gibbons v. Ogden* (1824) and *Charles River Bridge v. Warren Bridge* (1837). More recently, growing prosperity and higher standards of living for the common man have inspired constitutional amendments widening the franchise.

Trade also soon led to changes in the society and economy that had political and constitutional implications for ancient Athens. From their trade with Asia, the Greeks learned to coin money. Instead of bartering, they started minting silver coins and imprinting them with the head of a god, much as we put the image of Washington or Jefferson, for example, on ours. In time, this cash economy made the society more fluid. Poor farmers who were not noble by birth could make things and exchange them for coins.

One of the first items these farmers bought when they had some money was armor. In America these days, when people make money, they go out and buy fancy clothes or a posh car. In ancient Greece, armor was the sign of success. It meant you could take your place in battle along with the nobles. Soon it became clear that it no longer took noble blood to defend the polis. People began asking the next obvious question: why should it take noble blood to rule the polis? In our case, it was surely no accident that the suffrage was expanded to eighteen-to-twenty-one-year-olds when people that age were being drafted to go to Vietnam. "Old enough to fight, old enough to vote" was the cry. In ancient Greece, "wealthy enough to fight, wealthy enough to rule" became the slogan of the day.

All this started to produce growing class strife and popular discontent. Eager for a "fair deal," the poor demanded first that the laws be written down—much as the anti-Federalists demanded a written

Bill of Rights in 1789—so they could know what they could do and what they could not. The nobles finally acceded.

From a legal point of view, the first important development in Athens was the publication, around 620 BC, of a code of laws by Draco. These laws moved Athens away from vendettas and private vengeance and toward public justice. They were very harsh, however. They mandated the death penalty for practically every crime and were thus said to be "written in blood."

Still, they were rich men's laws. The poor of Athens demanded debt relief, freedom from slavery, and land redistribution. Class warfare brought Athens to the point where each side, rich and poor, agreed to the appointment of a dictator in order to settle the situation. This dictator was Solon.

Solon was a poet and a merchant, a man descended from the ancient kings but only moderately rich. He was chosen because he was respected by both rich and poor. In his constitutional and political reforms, he tried to balance the interests of both sides.

Constitutionally, Solon mixed aspects of oligarchy (rule of the rich) and democracy (rule of the poor). For example, he gave the people more power by enabling them to participate in the assembly and elect the magistrates, but he insisted that the magistrates be drawn from only the upper classes.

Our constitutional system can also be understood as a mix of oligarchy and democracy. Its oligarchic features are evident in the power that money and big corporations wield in American politics. On the other hand, we have democratic elections and one-person, one-vote. Members of Congress and the president still have to run for office and for reelection, paying attention to the will of the electorate.

Unlike the Constitution of our Founding Fathers, however, Solon's reforms did not last. Like Washington, Solon refused to make himself king. He left office, and left Athens, having set up the constitution and bound the people by oath to abide by it. But as soon as he left, the people started quarreling again, and Athens soon fell into the hands of the tyrant Pisistratus.

For us the term *tyrant* generally means a malevolent, cruel dictator—a Hitler, Stalin, or Saddam Hussein. For the Greeks, the word signified a man who had seized power without any constitutional authority. It implied no negative judgment about the person. Pisistratus—who ruled Athens from about 560 to about 530 BC—was a kind of benevolent tyrant. With bodyguards armed with clubs, he seized power, which he used to preserve the forms of Solon's moderately democratic constitution. As Aristotle would later say, "he wished to govern according to the laws without any prerogatives." Economically, Pisistratus improved the lot of the poor. Legally, he broke once and for all the political monopoly of the nobles. From then on, the government of Athens came under the law.

When Pisistratus died, he was succeeded by his sons, but eventually the tyranny failed. Although the nobles tried to abolish the reforms, the Athenians rose up against them and, in what has been described as the first democratic revolution, took back the city. Another noble, Cleisthenes, took power and, like the framers of the post-reconstruction Civil War amendments and twentieth-century changes in the American Constitution, he completed the democratizing revolution that Solon and Pisistratus had begun.

Cleisthenes helped break the old power of the tribes and made it easier to become a citizen. He also introduced ostracism: the assembly could propose that a citizen should go into exile on the grounds that his mere presence there was a threat to the constitution. If six thousand citizens agreed to this, the man named had to leave Athens for ten years. This was not really a public disgrace, but like our Twenty-Second Amendment limiting presidents to two terms, it was a deterrent to political ambition.

These reforms of Solon, Pisistratus, and Cleisthenes gave Athens a more or less democratic constitution. The Greek world continued for awhile in relative peace, with great empires rising and falling elsewhere without so much as a ripple of anxiety in Greek minds. In time, however, events started to prove that even the Greeks could not live in isolation.

America found itself in the same isolationist position in the late nineteenth century. As the great classical historian Eduard Meyer pointed out, it was the American decision to go to war with Spain in 1898 that was the turning point. This war was closely followed by American involvement in World War I, and it might truly be said that it was not until World War II that the Americans learned the lesson the Greeks had learned from the Persian Wars: "that, whatever their personal preference might be, no people could live in seclusion or entirely unto itself."[3]

A civil libertarian is tempted to say that, in learning that lesson, America has created a situation in which the worst threats to our Constitution emerge, all too often, from our propensity to favor security over liberty and thus bring about the erosion of our constitutional rights. The Korematsu case, in which the Supreme Court upheld the relocation of Japanese Americans on the West Coast of the United States as a necessary measure during World War II, is often cited as an example of this erosion.

Still, it was not the Korematsu case that threatened our Constitution per se, but the world situation that prompted the United States government to respond with the Japanese relocation policy. Put more directly, it was World War II in general and the Japanese attack on Pearl Harbor in particular that threatened the U.S. Constitution.

Lincoln understood that the Constitution he swore to "preserve, protect, and defend" was far more than just a document or a collection of rights and liberties. The Constitution, Lincoln reminds us in his First Inaugural Address, is nothing less than the nation itself—a nation for which the written Constitution is an organic law.

Understood in this way, the gravest threats to the American Constitution in our history have been the threats to our nation. The most serious of those was, of course, the Civil War. In the 1930s, the Great Depression also posed a significant threat. Threats from overseas, however, were a different matter.

As late as the 1930s, Americans continued to see themselves as isolated from the events of the world. Our nation had, to be sure, fought Spain in the war of 1898, and we had entered World War I to "make the world safe for democracy." But, after that war, we had rejected Wilson's League of Nations and fallen back on the habits of isolationism.

It was World War II—and particularly the Japanese attack on Pearl Harbor—that jolted us out of our complacent isolationism, just as the attacks of 9/11 taught us once and for all that we are not always safe on our own shores.

The great Greek historian of Rome Polybius taught us more than two thousand years ago that there comes a time in the development of a nation when it moves beyond isolationism to aspire to a more active participation in the affairs of the world. After a people has passed from rule of one to rule of few to rule of many, Polybius says, it begins to shed its isolationist past and take a greater interest in world events.

By the time the United States moved on to the world scene in the Spanish American War and then the two world wars, our Constitution had evolved from the rule of one to the rule of few to the rule of many. So, too, had the Athenian constitution by the time of the Persian Wars. Prior to those wars, the Athenians were relatively content in their isolationism. But the Persian threat reminded them that the barbarians around them were not Greek and not ruled by law. It taught them that, as Stringfellow Barr puts it, "none save only Zeus is free."[4]

The Persian Wars were the greatest and most difficult test of the new democratic constitution that Cleisthenes had won for Athens. As the Greek historian Herodotus tells us, the eventual victory of the Greeks was the triumph of freedom over despotism. Another modern historian echoes this theme:

> Greece had stemmed the tide of Oriental despotism and opened for Europe a destiny of free intellectual life.... Already Greece had mapped her course along the path of free institutions, constitutional government, freedom of the intellect, and the supremacy of law and reason, while Persia epitomized the

arbitrary despotism of an Oriental autocracy over obsequious subjects. The defeat of Persia assured freedom to the western world for twenty-five hundred years.[5]

This may seem an exaggeration. But for Athens, the defeat of the Persians was an historic turning point, the equivalent of our victory over Fascism in World War II. After the Battles of Salamis and Platea, the Athenians must have felt as the British did, standing in front of Buckingham Palace on the day Nazi Germany surrendered, to hear Winston Churchill thunder from the balcony: "This is your victory. We have never had a greater day than this!" For the Greeks in general and the Athenians in particular, victory over the Persians meant the triumph of their democratic constitution and, indeed, of their democratic way of life.

As for the American "democratic way of life," we have seen that our Founding Fathers introduced many democratic features in the Constitution of 1787. They also sought to combine reliance on the people with checks on mob passion, however. For example, they specified in Article VI, and later again in Amendment VI, that criminal trials would be by jury. They visualized a division of responsibility at the trial court level between aristocratic judges, appointed at the federal level for life, and democratically selected juries.

Some of these kinds of specific constitutional compromises between aristocracy and democracy have direct parallels in the constitutional development of ancient Athens. Solon, for instance, also took away some of the powers of the Areopagus—the aristocratic law court whose divine origins were celebrated years later by Aeschylus in his *Eumenide*—and introduced the popular law court, or Heliaea, which was elected by the people and served as a court of appeal from the decisions of the magistrates. It was Cleisthenes who later strengthened this court. Juries, chosen by lot, numbered as many as a thousand and no fewer than a hundred. Anyone could bring a case against anyone else, whether he was the aggrieved party or not; there was no concept of standing as there is in our law. Also unlike our law, there were no lawyers. The litigants or parties to the case had to plead their own cases personally. They could rely on professional speechwriters, but the litigant had to learn his speech by heart and make the speech himself. Rhetorical skill was highly prized, as the jury—which preferred to ignore precedent and decide each case on its own—settled not only the guilt or innocence of the accused but also the penalty, all by secret ballot.

In the years after the Battle of Marathon and the defeat of the Persians, the aristocratic Areopagus was stripped of its powers except the right to decide homicide cases—still considered religious offenses of impiety. Jurymen were now paid for their services, permitting all citizens, rich and poor, to serve.

Juries were thus a democratic feature of early America and of ancient Athens. For all their fondness for democracy, however, our Founding Fathers worried about majority tyranny. One important restraint on popular sovereignty was, of course, worked out in the first important case the Supreme Court handed down. In *Marbury v. Madison* (1803), Chief Justice Marshall established the principle of judicial review, the power of the court to declare acts of legislatures unconstitutional.

The ancient Athenians found a similar solution. To prevent their mass assembly from degenerating into a mob, swayed by the passionate appeals of a demagogue, and to guard against rash changes in the law, the Athenians adopted what has sometimes been called a writ of illegality. Any person who proposed a new law could be sued in the courts for proposing an unconstitutional law. If he was acquitted, the law was passed; if not, the proposer was punished by the jury. This innovation discouraged rash legal proposals but also forced a sober second look at the law.

There was apparently no definite criterion for determining when a law was unconstitutional, but the proposer would try to convince the jury that it was consistent with past laws and customs. This is not quite our concept of judicial review, nor is it our sense of stare decisis and precedent, but it may be as close as the ancient world ever got.[6]

The American framers also made clear in the Constitution that there were to be no restrictions on who could serve in federal public office beyond the very limited ones of age, citizenship, and residence. Athens also allowed all citizens to participate.

Above all, Athenian democracy at its height was for amateurs. The whole constitutional system was based on the belief that every citizen who wanted to participate had a right to participate actively, and was capable of participating actively in the public affairs of the city. It has been said that, at any one time, nearly a sixth of the citizens were engaged in public activity of one kind or another—in juries and in administrative positions. There was, as the historian C. E. Robinson puts it, "the widest possible scope for the individual Athenian citizen to enjoy the privilege of political responsibility, and to gain experience of administrative practice."[7]

Administration soon fell to a board of ten "generals," and in time, one of those generals each year came to have preeminence over the rest. That general came to be regarded as a sort of president. For many years at the height of Athenian democracy, this president was a man named Pericles.

For all its democratization, the American Constitution in the twentieth century also concentrated power in the hands of one officer, the president. In much the same way, democratic Athens came to know one-man rule. Discussing Pericles in his *History of the Peloponnesian War*, Thucydides says Athens was only "called" a democracy. Despite its democratic constitution, in other words, Athens was in reality dependent on one man, Pericles. It was Pericles, of course, who famously inspired the Athenians to fight the great war with Sparta.

Constitutionally, Sparta was in some ways the antithesis of Athens. If Athens was a democracy, Sparta was an oligarchy with two constitutional monarchs. It was the stability of this constitutional system—a stability attributed to the legendary lawgiver Lycurgus—that Plato and other philosophers of antiquity as well as American Founders such as Madison admired.

In his life of Lycurgus, Plutarch tells us that his constitution reduced the "prerogative" of Spartan kings "within reasonable bounds," seeing to it that the class interests of the citizens effectively checked and balanced each other. Here in Sparta, not in Athens, then, was an early forerunner of our American checks and balances, so celebrated by Madison in *The Federalist Papers* as one of the great "auxiliary precautions."

The result was that, as Thucydides pointed out, having "never been ruled by tyrants," Sparta, unlike revolution-prone Athens, was able to preserve "the same system of government" for more than four hundred years. Thucydides does not hesitate to add that it was the excellence of Sparta's constitution that gave her "internal strength" and thus enabled her to "intervene in the affairs of other states."[8]

As for Athens, Thucydides recounts how events demonstrated the weakness of the Athenian democratic constitution in its dependence in time of crisis on one-man rule. It is well known that, at the lowest point in the war, the Athenian people, discouraged about the war and the plague and incited by rival politicians jealous of Pericles's power, charged Pericles with embezzlement. After a trial that is somewhat similar to the impeachment and trial of an American president such as Andrew Johnson or Bill Clinton, Pericles was stripped of power, found guilty, and fined a large sum of money. Soon after, the Athenians began to realize how much they needed Pericles and reinstated him. It was too late, however. Pericles had contracted the plague himself. After six months of lingering illness, he died.

With Pericles gone and the war still far from won, Athens floundered—much as the United States might have done if Lincoln had been assassinated before Union victory in the Civil War was assured or if FDR had died before Allied victory over Germany and Japan had begun to take shape. With no firm leader at the helm, Athenian democracy—which had a tendency to be, as we mentioned, not checked and balanced like the Spartan constitution or the American system, but rather a pure democracy—began to show its terrible tendency to slide into mob rule.

Eventually, this constitutional weakness paved the way for Athens'

defeat in the war with Sparta. With the support of the Spartan conquerors, a small oligarchic group of thirty men was selected to draw
up a new constitution for Athens. This group of "Thirty Tyrants" proceeded to usurp power for themselves. Like the French Republicans
after the 1793 execution of Louis XVI, these Thirty Tyrants embarked
on a reign of terror, executing nearly fifteen hundred Athenians.
Eventually, as in France hundreds of years later with the execution
of Robespierre, the most bloodthirsty of the rulers was killed, and, in
the case of Athens, democracy was restored. But compared with the
glory days of the golden age it was a changed democracy—an embittered democracy, and one that soon began looking for a scapegoat
to blame for Athens's terrible misfortunes. That scapegoat was, of
course, Socrates.

THREE

The Empire of Reason:
Socrates, Plato, and Aristotle

There can be no satisfactory account of the influence of ancient Greece on our constitutional system without a discussion of some of the seminal ideas of the three greatest Greek philosophers, the three "teachers" who first explained logic and applied it in every conceivable way: Socrates, whose words were recorded by his star pupil, Plato; Plato himself; and Aristotle, Plato's student, who explored not only the nature of government but also subjects ranging from poetry and rhetoric to plants and animals. These three men gave the Greeks an empire of ideas and masterpieces of thought, not of conquered lands and enslaved peoples. Our Founding Fathers saw in those ideas and in that heritage not just a model to follow but also the rational foundation for American constitutionalism.

The *Dialogues of Socrates*, recorded by Plato, are the first substantive writings in history that explore a philosophy of government and of the role of the citizen. In *Crito*, for example, we have Socrates's famous dialogue with the laws—a play within a play much like the one in Shakespeare's *Hamlet*. "Was this the agreement we had between us?" the laws ask Socrates as he contemplates escape from prison. This argument is mirrored in the social-contract theory of Hobbes and Locke and foreshadows our Declaration of Independence. In the end, the laws give Socrates an ultimatum: obey us or persuade us differently. Americans face a similar ultimatum time and time again: we can try to persuade our elected officials to change their policies if we disagree with them, but ultimately, if persuasion fails and we cannot vote them out of office, we have no choice, under the law, but to obey.

Does that mean that government is nothing more than the interest of the stronger? Is there no such thing as the national interest or national security—only elite interest and the rulers' security? Many modern commentators would answer yes to such questions.

So would many professors in our leading universities. Thrasymachus says as much in book 1 of Plato's *Republic*. So does Glaucon at the start of book 2, where he uses the story of the magic ring to make his point: that we would all prefer to do injustice if we could get away with it.

To appreciate the significance of this argument against justice, and, above all, to appreciate the importance of the Socratic response and its impact on American constitutional law, one must know the philosophical context in which this debate was launched in ancient times. Like many modern scientists searching for fixed and unchangeable laws to explain nature, the pre-Socratics of ancient Greece had taken on the same task. They were challenged soon enough by the Sophists, paid itinerant teachers of rhetoric, who held that there were no such immutable laws, and that justice and human law were rooted not in nature (*physis*) but rather in convention (*nomos*) and reflect "not an eternal, underlying reality, but arbitrary humanly constructed accommodations invented by people simply for reasons of convenience, tradition, or self-interest."[1] Truth itself is relative for the Sophists, who thought that truth depended on who was looking for it and in part on what interests would be served by believing in one theory versus another. Such a view came under sharp attack, first and most famously by Socrates, and then by Plato and Aristotle. Indeed, it is largely from these latter thinkers that words like *sophist* and *sophistry* received the negative connotations that they carry to this day.[2]

Our Supreme Court has accepted the Socratic approach to this subject. In case after case, the justices have made clear that there is such a thing as justice and that human laws and institutions can and should be judged against its unwavering standard. For example, in

Palko v. Connecticut in 1937, the Court, in explaining which Bill of Rights provisions apply to the states through due process, made much use of the language of natural justice derived from Plato. Justice Cardozo said that those rights which "have been found to be implicit in the concept of ordered liberty" are part of due process. Abolishing such rights, he says, would violate a "principle of justice so rooted in the traditions and conscience of our people as to be ranked as fundamental." The test of whether a criminal process violates due process, Cardozo wrote, is whether it violates "fundamental principles of liberty and justice which lie at the base of all our civil and political institutions." Similarly, in his famous concurring opinion a decade later in *Adamson v. California*, Justice Frankfurter also echoes Plato in referring to natural justice and to "those canons of decency and fairness which express the notions of justice of English-speaking peoples even toward those charged with the most heinous offenses."[3]

When the U.S. Supreme Court speaks of "canons of decency and fairness," its words cry out for comparison with what Socrates is saying about justice in the *Republic*. For Socrates and Plato and for the Court, there is such a thing as justice and it does have meaning.

These cases help show some of the modern relevance of Plato's utopian reflections. Despite his fundamental idealism, however, Plato proves in many of his writings that he is also a clear-thinking realist. In *The Laws*, he says that a mix of monarchy and democracy may be the best practical form of government. Our constitutional system with its president as a sort of monarch and its Congress as a semidemocratic institution may be considered a modern application of Plato's ideal. Also in *The Laws*, Plato says there will still need to be criminal laws and punishments—perhaps even the death penalty—even in a well-ordered state, because crime is an inevitable flaw in human nature.

The realism in Plato's late dialogues is also present, of course, in the writings of Plato's brilliant pupil Aristotle, the greatest philosopher the ancient world ever produced. Aristotle's *Ethics*, with its emphasis on individual responsibility and choice, is particularly relevant in understanding the philosophical foundations of our criminal law system.

Unlike the modern social scientist who teaches, quite in the spirit of Jean-Jacques Rousseau, that man is really a noble savage—inherently good by nature if only left to his own instincts and freed from the corruption of society—Aristotle says in the opening chapter of his *Ethics*, book 2, that moral virtue does not come to us by nature. We are not born morally good. If we were, he goes on, this moral virtue could not be changed by practice, just as the nature of a stone to fall to the ground when dropped cannot be altered by practice. Since repetition of morally virtuous acts makes us more morally virtuous, and repetition of morally vicious acts makes us more morally vicious, it follows for Aristotle that we are not born morally virtuous. Instead, we learn moral virtue by practice, by developing the right habits.

Aristotle believed that words alone "do not have the capacity to turn the common run of people to goodness and nobility" because people "refrain from acting basely not because it is disgraceful but because of the punishment it brings." For Aristotle, we get good habits from good laws. A person learns to play the harp by practicing the harp, but he or she will not practice well without a good instructor. Similarly, Aristotle says, we learn to practice moral virtue under the guidance of good government and good laws.

In book 3 of *Ethics*, Aristotle turns to a new although related subject that is of great significance to our law. He says that virtue is about feelings and actions, but feelings and actions are only praised or blamed if they are voluntary. We do not praise or blame someone for something that is involuntary. The definition of voluntariness, he says, is particularly important for legislators, who must assign rewards and punishments only to voluntary acts.

It is important to note that our own modern criminal law also assumes that an act must be voluntary before it can be subject to criminal punishment. The drafters of the Model Penal Code are as emphatic as Aristotle on the subject: "A person is not guilty of an offense unless his liability is based on conduct which includes a voluntary act or the omission to perform an act of which he is physically capable."

The drafters of the code explained the reason for this rule in their commentary, basing their argument on the purposes of punishment. The law, they said, "cannot hope to deter involuntary movement or to stimulate action that cannot physically be performed....People whose involuntary movements threaten harm to others may present a public health or safety problem calling for therapy or even for custodial commitment; they do not present a problem of correction."[4]

Aristotle would probably say that this comment would be clarified immeasurably if "correction" in that last line were changed to "punishment." It is because the purpose of criminal law is to punish—not just to correct—that it makes sense to apply it only to voluntary actions.

Plato makes a similar distinction in his *Apology of Socrates*, where he has Socrates answer his accuser Meletus by saying that, if he is corrupting the youth, he must be doing so unwillingly and therefore he should not be charged as a criminal: "Now if I corrupt them unwillingly, the law does not require you to bring people to court for such unwilling wrongdoings, but to get hold of them privately, to instruct them and exhort them...but you bring me here, where the law requires one to bring those who are in need of punishment, not of instruction."[5]

For Aristotle, then, only voluntary actions are the subject of criminal law because criminal law is about punishment and only voluntary actions can be punished or blamed. American courts adopt this same view, even to the point of reading the requirement of voluntariness into a statute when it is not expressly written there.

Our law also distinguishes between coerced acts and acts done through mistake. Aristotle similarly says that there are two main ways in which an act can be truly involuntary: if the act is done "by force" or if the act is done "because of ignorance." An action done "by force," for Aristotle, occurs when the person contributes nothing—for example, a wind blows your hand into someone's face, or someone picks you up and carries you.

A more difficult case arises, Aristotle says, with actions done because of fear of greater evils. For example, if a thief puts a knife to your throat and demands money, your action of giving it to him, Aristotle would say, is mostly voluntary. Even though you most certainly would not have given him the money had he not threatened your life, still it was your hand that reached in the pocket and handed him the money.

Our criminal law follows this Aristotelian reasoning by limiting involuntary actions—or what criminal lawyers call "non actions"—to spasms and reflexes for which the defendant has no responsibility whatever. The Model Penal Code gives examples of involuntary acts, some of which Aristotle would have recognized:

a reflex or convulsion

a bodily movement during unconsciousness or sleep

conduct during hypnosis or resulting from hypnotic suggestion

a bodily movement that is not a product of the effort or determination of the actor, either conscious or habitual.[6]

If a person has a sudden and unexpected fit while driving a car, for instance, and hits another person with his vehicle, most English and American courts recognize a complete defense of "automatism" or "lack of actus reus [guilty act]," because they say there was no voluntary act on his part. But an action done because of fear of a greater evil is still considered voluntary. Let us say, for example, that a person is threatened with death if he does not kill or rape another person. If he does kill or rape, the law will regard this as a voluntary action.

It is important to recognize that, for Aristotle, as for modern criminal law, lack of voluntary action is definitely not the same thing as inability to control a strong impulse. The English jurist Lord Denning explained this distinction in one of his rulings:

No act is punishable if it is done involuntarily; and an involuntary act in this context...means an act which is done by the muscles without any control by the mind such as a spasm, a reflex action, or a convulsion.... [But an act is not] to be regarded as an involuntary act simply because the doer could not control his impulse to do it. When a man is charged with murder, and it appears that he knew what he was doing but he could not resist it, then his assertion, "I couldn't help myself" is no defense in itself.[7]

Another distinction our law makes that Aristotle would certainly recognize is one between non acts (involuntary movements) and excused acts. An act that is done mistakenly, accidentally, by compulsion, or under duress may well be an excused act, and may be subject to less or no criminal punishment. But it is still a voluntary act.

When can mental illness be a defense in criminal law? Aristotle takes up that question in the rest of chapter 1, book 3 of his *Ethics*. He says there is a difference between actions "caused by ignorance" and actions done "in ignorance." Acting "because of ignorance" is involuntary and may be pardoned. But if we act "in ignorance," then something besides the ignorance is the cause of our action, and we may be held responsible. For instance, a drunk who kills someone while driving is acting in ignorance; his ignorance was caused by his drunkenness. Aristotle would say that he is at fault for that drunkenness. The same reasoning is behind our own law, which does not accept drunkenness as a defense for vehicular homicide.

Aristotle goes on in the same passage to talk about ignorance of the universal and ignorance of the particulars. Imagine the following syllogism or logical argument:

1. This piece of personal property (a hat, for instance) belongs to someone else;

2. it is wrong to take something that belongs to someone else;

3. I must not take this item.

Aristotle says that if you do not know the first premise—you do not know that this is someone else's hat, for instance—then you might be excused, depending on the circumstances. But if you don't know the second premise—if you don't know that it is wrong to take something that belongs to someone else—then you are wicked. Ignorance in moral choice, Aristotle says emphatically, does not make an act excusable. It is, in fact, a definition of vice.

It is important to see that the same principle applies today in our criminal law. We do sometimes allow a defense of mistake of fact if a person was not aware of some important fact—for instance, if he did not know that a hat belonged to someone else. But we would never allow someone accused of theft to defend himself by saying he did not know it was wrong to steal! We would never allow someone accused of murdering to defend by saying he did not know it was wrong to kill!

In discussing what we would call mistake of fact, Aristotle lists some of the particulars of which a person might be unaware: he might not know "what he is doing; about what or to what he is doing it; sometimes also what he is doing it with." Someone who accidentally shoots another person in the woods with a gun might be unaware that the gun is loaded, or he might be unaware that the figure in his sights is a human being, not an animal. If he is ignorant of all the particulars, Aristotle says, we would have to call him mad.

Modern criminal law, of course, has a defense of insanity. The famous M'Naughten version of this defense says a person is insane if, because of mental disease or defect, he did not know what he was doing or he did not know that what he was doing was wrong.

This test appears to allow people to defend by saying they did not know that what they were doing was wrong—the very point on which Aristotle was so adamant. And yet this insanity defense is really not at odds with what Aristotle is saying. It is only when we have a mental disease or defect and also do not, because of that disease or defect, know that what we are doing is wrong that we can be excused under this approach.

If Aristotle were asked to evaluate a modern claim of criminal insanity, he might ask what caused the mental disease or defect. If a person was born insane, for instance, that would clearly not be his or her fault. But if a person, through long indulgence in drugs or alcohol, made himself insane, that would, in Aristotle's view, be quite a different matter.

Leaving the subject of the voluntary and involuntary in chapter 2 of book 3, Aristotle turns to choice. Voluntariness, he asserts, is a broader term than choice. Children and animals can engage in voluntary acts, but not choice. Choice, he says, is not the same thing as wishing or as belief or opinion. Choice involves deliberation. We deliberate about things that are in our power—about means, not about ends. A doctor deliberates about how to make his patient well, not whether to make him well. A lawyer deliberates about how to win her case, not whether to win her case.

A murderer may deliberate about whether to kill his victim. One of the ways in which American states tend to distinguish first- from second-degree murder is by asking whether there was a "willful, premeditated, and deliberate" killing. Justice Cardozo once said that the phrase "'willful, premeditated, and deliberate' is so obscure that no jury hearing it…can fairly be expected to…understand it." Some courts use these three terms interchangeably.

One wonders what Aristotle would understand by our term *deliberate murder*. In English, the verb *deliberate* means "to consider or think carefully." Juries deliberate. The adjective *deliberate* means "careful, unhurried, or cautious." In the school desegregation cases, the Supreme Court ordered the desegregation to proceed "with all deliberate speed," meaning carefully and not too fast.

When describing murder, it is hard to see what the word *deliberate* adds beyond premeditated. If premeditated murder means a murder that was thought about before hand, what does a deliberate murder mean? One recent article tries to make the distinction: "It has been suggested that for premeditation, the killer asks himself, 'Shall I kill him?'... The deliberation part of the crime requires a thought like, 'Wait, what about the consequences? Well, I'll do it anyway.'"[8]

The concept of deliberation and choice is absolutely central to Aristotle's ethical philosophy. It is central to our criminal law, of course, as well. Choice makes us responsible for the things we do, and blameworthy if we do wrong. Aristotle clearly thinks we are responsible. We choose certain actions, he says. Over time, those actions become habits. The habits shape our character. If we do good things, in time we become better or virtuous. If we habitually do bad things, in time we become bad. Either way we are responsible because we made the initial choice to perform the good or bad acts.

This is completely different from Plato's perspective. Plato insists that vice is involuntary. Virtue, he says, produces happiness and vice produces unhappiness. No one would rationally desire to be unhappy. From this, it follows for Plato that, if someone does practice vice (does bad things), it must be because he does not know that he is doing bad things. Hence, vice is caused by ignorance. Vice is involuntary.

To all this, Aristotle has but one response: VICE IS VOLUNTARY! It is possible, he thinks, to know what is good and still do what is bad. It is the choice that makes us responsible and at fault.

In this way, Aristotle is much closer to our criminal law than Plato is. If we looked on all vice as involuntary, we really could not punish people for doing anything. Punishment implies responsibility and choice. This is Aristotle's legacy to our criminal law.

Consider some of the examples Aristotle himself gives. He says that "legislators impose corrective treatment for the ignorance itself, if the agent seems to be responsible for the ignorance. A drunk, for instance, pays a double penalty,... since he controls whether he gets drunk and his getting drunk causes his ignorance." In our criminal law, intoxication is rarely an excuse for crime. In fact, it often worsens it. Aristotle also speaks of a man who is "in ignorance of some provision of the law that he is required to know and that it is not hard to know." Such a man has no excuse for that ignorance. In our law, too, it is well known that "ignorance of the law is not an excuse."

Finally, Aristotle speaks of a careless or negligent person. He is, Aristotle explains, "responsible for becoming this sort of person because he has lived carelessly." Our law takes the same view. We do not allow someone charged with reckless driving to defend by saying that it is his nature to be careless. We tend to assume that, even if people are extremely careless, they became that way due to their own fault.

Of course, not all commentators on the law agree that we should be so harsh. Rehabilitationists see the purpose of punishment as correction—getting the accused to see the error of their ways. Unlike modern criminal rehabilitationists, who often take the view that criminal law and the need to punish would radically decrease if we improved society, Aristotle insists that "just punishments" are a necessary evil: "they are good only because we cannot do without them [and] it would be better that neither individuals nor states should need anything of the sort."

In other words, like the framers of our Constitution in general and the authors of *The Federalist Papers* in particular, Aristotle was fundamentally pessimistic about man's capacity to be good without the restraining force of law. Man, he says in *Politics*, is the worst of animals when separated from the coercive restraints of law and justice. That is why man is a political animal—a creature who reaches his potential only in the polis.

Much else in *Politics* speaks to us today. There is, for example, Aristotle's praise for politics as the master science and for the state as the highest form of association that aims at the highest good. We might do well to take that passage to heart in these days when *the state* and *politics* have become ugly words. There is also Aristotle's famous defense of the family as a natural human institution. One wonders what Aristotle would say about same-sex marriage laws.

Politics also contains Aristotle's critique of Plato's communism, and as good a defense of private property as any in Locke or any found in British or American common law. People work harder, Aristotle says, for what is their own. This simple but elegant argument lies behind the case for lower taxes and for private ownership of land. It lies behind our Constitution's copyright clause, which permits Congress to award temporary monopolies to inventors and creators in order to give them an incentive to create. And it lies behind some of the most famous property cases in the history of American law.

In addition to his remarks about property, there is Aristotle's account of citizenship in book 3 of *Politics*, where he makes clear that he would fundamentally disagree with our Constitution's statement that citizenship is a birthright of all those born in the United States and subject to its jurisdiction. Not all who are born in or live in Athens or any city-state are citizens, Aristotle avers. Citizenship, he says, means sharing in office. A citizen rules and prepares the ruled to rule in turn. Just as there are different types of good citizen, so there are, Aristotle says, different types of constitution. And not all are equal in quality. Those constitutions that look to the common good are preferable, Aristotle says, to those that aspire only to the well-being of the rulers. Our foreign policy in the two world wars and the cold war, as well as our policy today in the war on terror, is built on a similar assumption.

In the end, then, in his emphasis on the virtues of rule of the middle class, in his stress on the virtues of a mixed regime of both democratic and oligarchic elements—of both rule of the poor and rule of the rich—and in his preference for the rule of law tempered by equity to correct the generality and harshness of law, Aristotle is the supremely modern ancient philosopher. But what became of the ancient Greece and ancient Athens that had given rise to such brilliant philosophy? The story is long and painful—a story of defeat and disgrace, of collapse and humiliation. Eventually, the weakness of Athenian democracy left Athens prey to be swallowed up by more unified and politically powerful neighbors—first the Macedonians under King Philip II and Alexander the Great, and later the Romans, whose influence on our Constitution and way of life is the subject of the section that follows.

PART TWO

The Constitution of Ancient Rome

FOUR

Rome, America, and the Importance of Roman Law

Ancient Roman history is remarkably similar to our own. Founded according to legend in 753 BC, Rome by 600 BC was a prosperous city-state on a river, governed by a monarchy. A hundred years later, the monarchy had been overthrown and a republic inaugurated, in much the same way that the English monarchy was cast off and an American republic was founded in our early history. By 270 BC, Rome was in command of a huge confederacy of the whole of the Italian peninsula south of Genoa, much as America had come to dominate the North American continent by the mid-1800s. A century and a half of wars later, Rome was a superpower—like twentieth- and twenty-first–century America—the only great power in the Mediterranean, the true successor to the empire of Alexander. By the death of the Roman Emperor Trajan in AD 117, the Roman Empire "stretched from Scotland to the Sudan, from the Atlantic coast of Portugal to the Caucuses—an area two-thirds the size of the continental United States of today, with perhaps a little less than half its population." That empire survived, in the West, until AD 476, when it continued in the East, its center Constantinople, until 1453, more than two thousand years after Rome was founded and only two generations before the discovery of the New World by a native of Italy, Christopher Columbus.[1]

Many writers have marveled at this phenomenal history and the fascinating parallel to our own national development. As Cullen

Murphy reminds us in his 2008 book *Are We Rome?*, the comparison between America and Rome "is by now so familiar, so natural, that...it comes to mind unbidden, ...for instance, in offhand references to welfare and televised sports as 'bread and circuses' or to illegal immigrants as 'barbarian hordes'...[or to] political pollsters as latter-day versions of Rome's oracles,...[or to] an 'imperial presidency' or to the president's aides as a 'Praetorian Guard.'"[2]

Nor is the comparison something new. Our Founding Fathers were constantly calling up Roman history as a model, both to emulate and to avoid. When asked what form of government had been set up at the Constitutional Convention, Benjamin Franklin replied, "a republic, if you can keep it"—a reminder that Rome, too, had a republic that eventually failed. In *The Federalist Papers*, Alexander Hamilton warned against having two presidents like the two consuls of the Roman Republic, who each took command of the army on alternate days, resulting in the military disaster at Cannae.

Murphy points out that an "obsession with Roman antecedents could hardly have been helped, given the classical education all the Founding Fathers received." These were, no doubt, all men who had been steeped in Roman history.

The virtues of Roman republican statesmen provided a moral standard for American statesmen. George Washington, Murphy points out, "was the epitome of America's Roman ideal." Supplementing Roman public virtue with his famous "Rules of Civility," Washington arranged for his frostbitten troops at Valley Forge to view a production of Joseph Addison's tragedy *Cato*, a play about Cato the Younger, the Roman republican hero and great-grandson of the Cato who had urged Rome to destroy Carthage in the Third Punic War. When, after the Revolution, Washington refused to make himself a king and retired to Mount Vernon, his contemporaries hailed him as the American equivalent of Cincinnatus, the Roman farmer of the fifth century BC who had famously put down his plough to serve as dictator when Rome needed him, then, his work accomplished, had laid down his sword and returned to his farm. We are reminded of this

Roman virtue by Gilbert Stuart's portrait of Washington, where our first president is depicted in the "serene mask of obligation," as well as by the massive marble statue immortalizing Washington in the classic Roman pose at the entrance to the Smithsonian Institution.[3]

The eyes of our Founders were clearly on the Roman Republic— imitating its rise and avoiding its fall. Today, as Murphy tells us, the "focus is not mainly on the Roman Republic but as much or more on the empire that took the republic's place." Comparisons between Rome's empire and our own, however, can proceed from a variety of perspectives. Some so-called "triumphalists," for example, "see America as at long last assuming its imperial responsibilities, bringing about a global Pax Americana like the Pax Romana of Rome at its most commanding." Other "declinists" warn of "imperial overstretch," and contend that, as with Rome, "our military and globalist ambitions exceed our capacity to pay for them." Still others warn of America in decline, like Rome, predicting a "new 'post Roman' era of medieval chaos and woe."[4]

There are, of course, important similarities between our own civilization and that of ancient Rome. Both America and Rome "are the most powerful actors in their worlds, by many orders of magnitude." Both are societies composed of many ethnicities and both have "created global structures—administrative, economic, military, cultural—that the rest of the world...take for granted." Both "revel in engineering prowess and grandiosity."[5]

The differences are no less significant, however. Rome, in its thousands of years of history, never left the Iron Age, while America moved from a primarily agricultural society through the Industrial Revolution and into the computer age and beyond. Rome remained a slaveholding society, with no significant middle class; America ultimately cast off slavery, and the predominance of a middle class is central to our social makeup. And then there are differences of attitude, which Murphy summarizes:

> I'm not sure that Americans, cast suddenly back in time, would ever warm to second-century Rome, the way they might to

Samuel Johnson's London.... Roman officials would unhesitat-
ingly commit suicide in situations [perhaps like our failure to
protect the Libyan embassy in 2012] that wouldn't make Americans even sit down with Barbara Walters.... If the past is another
country, then Rome is another planet. And yet, that planet colonized the one we inhabit now.[6]

Examining the similarities and differences between Rome and
America is not our primary reason for studying ancient Rome, however. British classical historian David Dudley has explained vividly
the debt that America and the West owe to Rome: "The intrinsic
interest of these twelve centuries of Roman history is in itself a claim
to the attention of all intelligent men. But there is something more.
The legacy of Rome in political institutions, in law, in language, in
religion, in literature, and the arts, and in much else besides has been
an enduring and perhaps indestructible part of the fabric of western civilization. We must understand Rome if we are to understand
ourselves."[7]

Roman Law and Its Influence on the Modern World

Looking at Rome with an eye to understanding ourselves in general
and the American constitutional tradition in particular requires
above all that we look at Roman law. As judge Hans Julius Wolff con-
tends in his *Roman Law: An Historical Introduction*, "Roman law
occupies a unique place in the history of our civilization."[8] It is the
greatest enduring Roman contribution to our world.

The ancient Greeks and the Athenians in particular gave us philosophy, drama, astronomy, history, and much else, but the Romans
gave us law. The late classical scholar Henry Paolucci contrasted the
Greek and Roman perspectives: "Roman law was the great Roman
contribution, the vehicle that expressed the meaning of Rome. If the
Greek was asked what the vehicle of expression of his meaning was,

he would point to the explanations of Thucydides, Aristotle, or Plato; the Roman would point to his laws, for they represent exactly what the Romans did."[9] In practically all intellectual disciplines, the Romans were the pupils of the Greeks; in law, as Barry Nicholas of Oxford reminds us, "they were, and knew themselves to be, the masters."[10]

Like Rome's political history, the history of Roman law is a remarkable story. It is perfectly accurate to say that Roman law has had two lives. The first began when Rome was a small rural community, continued as Rome expanded, and eventually became the law of a vast empire, embracing virtually the whole known world. This first history of Roman law was summarized and brought to an end in the reign of the Emperor Justinian in the sixth century.

The second life of Roman law began five and a half centuries after Justinian, when Roman law books came once again to be studied, this time in northern Italy, at first in universities like Bologna and later on in the courts of law. This second life of Roman law "exerted a deep influence on the development of legal institutions and doctrine in all continental European countries inside and outside the Empire, from Spain to Poland." It "gave to almost the whole of Europe a common stock of legal ideas, a common grammar of legal thought, and, to a varying but considerable extent, a common mass of legal rules."[11]

England alone held out against the tidal wave. Partly because of the early emergence of a common law and the early development of a legal profession trained in the Inns of Court rather than in the universities, England resisted the trend of Romanization of law that was dominating the universities of Europe in the Renaissance. For this reason, there are today two families of law that come from Europe. One is the common law of England and the English-speaking world, including, of course, the United States. The other is what comparative law scholars call the civil law, which is rooted in ancient Roman law and has influenced the law of almost every current European country and of former European colonies throughout the world.

There are, therefore, practical reasons to know the development of Roman law. The modern American lawyer who wants to communicate with a European or South American lawyer, for instance, simply must know something about Roman law. As Wolff reminds us, "modified forms of Roman law are even now the law of the land in Scotland, in Ceylon, and in the Union of South Africa (where it is called the Roman Dutch law)."[12] In France and former colonies of France, Roman law is extremely important because it greatly influenced the Napoleonic Code, which in turn is largely responsible for the codes of such places as Louisiana and Quebec as well as France. Knowledge of Roman law, then, "provides the Common lawyer with a key to the common language of almost every other system of law which traces its origin to Europe."

From the perspective of American law, however, the really important question is how Roman law influenced our constitutional system. An examination of four important ways in which the Roman legal world has had a lasting impact on American law—through legal formalism, legal realism, natural law, and the idea of a mixed constitution—can be followed by a short analysis of some similarities and differences between Roman law and our own). The discussion can help establish the relevance of studying Roman constitutional history in understanding our own legal system.

The Impact of Roman Law on the American Legal System

American law today is dominated by two jurisprudential perspectives: formalism and realism. The formalists, led by Christopher Columbus Langdell of Harvard in the late nineteenth century, taught that law is a scientific system and that correct answers to legal questions can be deduced mathematically from first principles. Our legal system today owes a great debt to the formalists. Law today remains, to a large extent, a scientific and systematic subject, with its own language, its own libraries, its own treatises, and its own logic.

This idea of law as a science and as a system is primarily Roman in its origins. The ancient Greeks, of course, had laws, and Plato and Aristotle give us comprehensive theories of law and its place in society. There was, as yet, however, no systematic study of law. The Romans gave us that study. Barry Nicholas of Oxford tells us that, in the hands of the Romans, "law became for the first time a thoroughly scientific subject, an elaborately articulated system of principles abstracted from the detailed rules which constitute the raw material of law."[13]

The story of how this scientific system emerged is itself an interesting one. In the Roman Republic, ministers of justice called praetors often lacked any legal expertise, so they increasingly turned to men who were learned in law to assist them. Gradually, it became customary for the leaders among these jurists to offer legal opinions (*responsa*) in public. At first these jurists were rich men from the top patrician families. By the late Republic, they were increasingly specialists in law, some of whom were from very humble backgrounds and thus would accept pay for their work. The modern legal profession was being born.

These legal opinions were compiled into longer works. In time, vast treatises on law were composed, and ultimately libraries of legal scholarship began to emerge. Near the end of the first life of Roman law, around AD 500, the emperor Justinian ordered a great compilation of all this accumulated material on law. It was this act that much later made possible the reception of Roman law in medieval Europe and consequently helps to explain the influence Roman law has had on the world.

The codification process officially began only a few months after Justinian succeeded to the throne. The chief minister for the project was Tribonian, a man of great learning who, like our American framers, was well acquainted with the works of classical Roman jurists and who held a number of high offices including consul.

The first stage was the compiling and updating of all existing imperial legislation. The emperor later issued a series of decrees, abolishing some obsolete legal rules and resolving disputed questions of law. Justinian's subordinates then set to work on a monumental task—reading, excerpting, and amending the texts of thousands of books of Roman juristic literature. The project, planned for ten years, took only three. The result was the *Digest*, a legal encyclopedia that is usually taken to be the most important single source of Roman law.

Together with the *Digest*, Justinian promulgated the *Institutes*, an introductory textbook for law students, which was also given the force of law, as well as a new *Code* of law, which suspended all previous codes. The *Digest*, *Institutes*, and *Code* all make up what is called the *Corpus Juris* (Body of Law) of Justinian. The *Corpus Juris* illustrates how the Romans pioneered the idea of law as a system—an idea that influenced the legal formalists and in turn has greatly influenced modern American law.

The formalist perspective is only one side of modern American law, however. In the writings of Oliver Wendell Holmes and other early-twentieth-century legal scholars, a reaction to legal formalism emerged. The self-proclaimed "legal realists" taught that law is not a precise deductive science and that, as Holmes himself famously said, "the life of the law has not been logic. It has been experience." In the tradition of Walter Bagehot, the realists argued that it is necessary to strip away the literary theory of a nation's legal system and look at the living reality of law with all its imperfections.

Legal realism can be said to have its roots in Roman realism, and Roman realism can perhaps best be seen in the stories the Romans told about their own origins. It is significant to notice, for example, that the Romans said that the founders of their state, Romulus and Remus, had been raised by a wolf. Not a dove, but a wolf. A wolf is a ravenous, bloodthirsty creature that lives in packs and obeys no laws. The Romans bluntly acknowledged by this story that their city began in theft and bloodshed. Perhaps we, too, made a similar acknowledgment when we adopted a bird of prey, the bald eagle, as our national symbol.

It took Saint Augustine, one millennium after the origins of Rome, and Machiavelli, one millennium later, to remind us that all earthly states begin in theft. Our own is no exception. Our history begins with the destruction of the "Indians" (now "Native Americans") and the theft of their land. We can agree with our first great chief justice, John Marshall, who declared, from the bench, that discovery and conquest give a property right "which the courts of the conqueror cannot deny." We also cannot deny, however, that our country started with theft.

That is not to condemn America or our history. All earthly governments begin in theft. There can be no lawful beginning to politics. As Saint Augustine said, a political community is a necessary evil. It begins with a band of robbers who gain impunity.

Romulus and Remus, according to the Roman story, formed such a band of robbers. All seemed well until it became clear that they both wanted to rule. According to the Roman historian Livy—and later Machiavelli, who wrote great commentaries on Livy (*Discourses*) and whose influence on the American Founders is seldom fully appreciated—Romulus killed his brother Remus and made himself the founding father of Rome.

The realism of this story should astound us today. We are not especially honest about our own origins as a nation—perhaps because we, like Plato's Socrates, believe in the necessity of false myths for the sake of national unity. The Romans, however, were honest, in their history and in their law. Henry Paolucci elaborates:

> The Romans were the only people who have stories about their beginnings that are not hypocritical. How was Rome founded? The Roman would tell you. He would tell you that the founding father was a man who committed fratricide and the men that banded about him were outcasts from other tribes, bandits and thieves who had served time.... The Romans' ugly reality was told in their legends and stories. But they were the only people, not only to have an ugly reality, but also to have ugly laws. They were doubly ugly. They were honest about it.... When they said something, they meant it. If they said a man could run for office, then he could run for it. Therefore, it took a long time before

they got around to saying it, and they did not say it often. But when they said it, they meant it.[14]

This Roman realism lives on in the legal realist tradition of our law schools and universities. Students trained by legal realist scholars in those schools, of course, go on to become practicing attorneys and judges and thus influence the future course of American law.

Legal formalism and legal realism are thus two important perspectives on current American law that can be said to owe their origins to Roman law and the Roman attitude toward law and government. An even more important idea that dominates American law and can be traced back to Roman law is that of natural law.

As we have seen, Plato and Aristotle speak of natural justice. It was the Greek Stoics, however, who gave the world the concept of natural law, and it was the Roman Cicero who cast this concept in a form through which it would later influence American jurisprudence. As Edward S. Corwin emphasizes in his famous essay "The Higher Law Background of American Constitutional Law," natural law was Cicero's great contribution to American law.

In his *De Legibus* (*On Law*), Cicero cast natural law in universal terms:

> Law is the highest reason implanted in Nature, which commands what ought to be done and forbids the opposite.... But the most foolish notion of all is the belief that everything is just which is found in the customs or laws of nations. Would that be true even if those laws had been enacted by tyrants?... For justice is one; it binds all human society, and is based on one Law, which is right reason applied to command and prohibition. Whoever knows not this Law, whether it has been recorded in writing anywhere or not, is without Justice.[15]

Cicero expounds more fully on the universal and unchanging character of natural law in his *De Re Publica* (*Republic*): "True law is right reason in agreement with nature; it is of universal application, unchanging and everlasting; it summons to duty by its commands, and averts from wrongdoing by its prohibitions,...and it is impossible to abolish it entirely. We cannot be freed from its obligations by senate or people."[16]

Cicero's remarks about natural law stand at the head of a long natural law tradition in jurisprudence—a tradition that takes us through the development of English common law in the writings of Bracton, Saint Thomas More, Coke, Blackstone, and Locke, and, through their profound influence on America, to our own shores. And what of the American natural law tradition? That can be traced at least as far back as the Declaration of Independence. There, Jefferson speaks of "the Laws of Nature and Nature's God" and "truths" that are "self-evident." In the same way, "cases prior to the constitutional convention similarly make reference to principles of fundamental law."[17] In one case, Alexander Hamilton defended a British citizen for occupying private property during the Revolution. The defendant's actions, he said, were justified by natural law, and the New York courts were bound to honor these "universal" principles. In an early Supreme Court case, *Calder v. Bull*, Justice Samuel Chase made clear that the justices would continue to be guided by this natural law standard: "There are certain vital principles in our free Republican governments, which will determine and over-rule an apparent and flagrant abuse of legislative power.... An act of the legislature (for I cannot call it a law) contrary to the great principles of the social compact, cannot be considered a rightful exercise of legislative authority.... It is against all reason and justice."[18]

> It would seem quite unusual for a Supreme Court justice today to base his or her decision on natural law, notwithstanding the continued relevance of Aristotle's observation, in his *Rhetoric*, that an advocate resorts to natural law when arguments from written law seem likely to lose. Nevertheless, the idea of a universal law against which we measure existing human laws is very much alive and well in American jurisprudence today.

We see it in cases such as *Griswold v. Connecticut*, in which the Supreme Court struck down a Connecticut law banning the use and sale of contraceptives on the ground that the law violated principles of privacy and fairness that no legislature could infringe—natural principles protected in the "penumbra" of the Bill of Rights. We see it in countless other cases of what has come to be called "substantive due process," which means there are certain things government cannot do to individuals no matter how it does them or what procedures it uses. We see it also when there is talk of international war crimes tribunals, such as those that tried the Nazis at Nuremberg and those that have tried war criminals like Saddam Hussein in our own day.

We see it also, perhaps most importantly, in the rhetoric of what can, for want of a better term, be called a "Natural Law School" of constitutional interpretation. One of the leading proponents of this approach was the late Supreme Court justice William Brennan. In his 1985 speech at the Text and Teaching Symposium at Georgetown University, Justice Brennan showed his debt to the Ciceronian and Roman natural law tradition when he said that our "Constitution embodies the aspiration to social justice, brotherhood, and human dignity that brought this nation into being." For Brennan, it is "the very purpose of a Constitution—and particularly of the Bill of Rights—to declare certain values transcendent, beyond the reach of temporary political majorities." These values, based on principles of natural law and natural justice, form the core of an unwritten Constitution which, in Brennan's view, the Supreme Court must apply.[19]

It is undeniable, therefore, that the American natural law tradition owes much to ancient Rome and has greatly influenced our contemporary jurisprudence. The third most important influence of Roman law on our law is in the idea and practice of a mixed constitution. Greek historians and political thinkers from Herodotus to Aristotle had taught that the best regime was one that was not dominated by any particular faction or group. Plato praises a mix of monarchy and democracy in *The Laws*. Aristotle in his *Politics* says that the ideal mix is one of democracy, the rule of the poor, and oligarchy, the rule of the rich. For both Plato and Aristotle, the emphasis in on ensuring that no one economic class dominates the state.

It was, however, Polybius, the Greek historian of Rome, who transformed the idea of that class-based mix of the ancient Greeks into an institutional mix. More precisely, Polybius recognized that the Romans had achieved an institutional balance among the parts of their republic, with powers divided between consuls, Senate, and assemblies. Polybius tells us that this Roman mix was so successful that it would have been impossible for an outside observer to say whether the Roman system was monarchical, aristocratic, or democratic. Each of the parts of the Roman Republic checked and balanced, and was checked and balanced by, the others. The result was a moderate regime that was likely to slow down the inevitable cycle to which all states—even great Rome—are prone.

These same checks and balances, of course, are at the heart of our constitutional system. Madison explains it in the famous words of *Federalist* No. 51:

> To what expedient, then, shall we finally resort, for maintaining in practice the necessary partition of power among the several departments as laid down in the Constitution? The only answer that can be given is…by so contriving the interior structure of the government as that its several constituent parts may, by their mutual relations, be the means of keeping each other in their proper places.…But the great security against a gradual concentration of the several powers in the same department consists in giving to those who administer each department the necessary constitutional means and personal motives to resist encroachments of the others. The provision for defense must, in this, as in all other cases, be made commensurate to the danger of attack. Ambition must be made to counteract ambition.[20]

In sum, then, through their development of law as a scientific and systematic subject, through the realism of their perspective on law and government, through their use of the concept of natural law, and through their practical application of the mixed constitution theory, the Romans had a profound influence on American law. Beyond these important contributions, however, there are more particular comparisons that deserve to be explored between Roman law and modern American law.

FIVE

Roman Law and American Law:
Comparisons and Contrasts

If one looks at the United States Supreme Court building, or at the U.S. Capitol, or at hundreds of other public law buildings in America today, one is struck by an obvious similarity: they are all modeled on Roman buildings. In our Supreme Court building, which dates back only to the 1930s, one can find busts of former chief justices dressed in Roman togas. Great American jurists and statesmen are sometimes shown in statues and paintings wearing Roman attire or carrying Roman-style weapons.

All of this is not mere symbolism. Most of our legal vocabulary is Roman in origin. Words like *justice, judge, jurisprudence, equity, equitable, constitution, code, legislation, regulation,* and even *legal* all have Latin antecedents.

These similarities, however, mask important differences between ancient Roman law and our own. A look at two areas of law—litigation and procedure, on the one hand, and citizenship, status, and family law, on the other—will help highlight those differences.

Litigation and Procedure

It is well known that America is one of the most litigious societies in history. Commentators are amazed at how often and how easily Americans sue each other. Each year, between ten and twenty million civil cases are filed, costing a great deal in public and private time and money.[1] Was the same true in ancient Rome?

The Roman poet Horace asks in his *Epistles* a famous question: "Who is the good man?" His answer is that the good man must be willing, inter alia (among other things) to serve as a witness, act as a guarantor, and decide cases as a judge. All of these legal responsibilities were among the duties expected of the Roman citizen.

But what about suing? Could a Roman citizen be respectable and be a litigant in a legal case? Cicero once advised that litigation is to be avoided like the plague, and many Romans apparently took that sort of advice very seriously. Litigation was seen as undignified and harmful to reputation.[2] This was partly because of the abuse one would suffer as a litigant in court from one's opponent's advocate.

Lawyers in the United States are well acquainted with the art of cross-examination, one purpose of which is always to impeach the credibility of the opposing side's witness—to show that the witness has a bad memory, or has a motive to lie, or did not see or hear as well as he or she claims. But our law of evidence puts important limits on cross-examination that the Roman trials did not observe. In our courts, cross-examination generally must be limited to the subject matter of direct examination, and an attorney may not, in direct or cross-examination, ask questions that assume facts not in evidence. For instance, one cannot suddenly ask, "When did you stop beating your wife?" if there is no evidence of any wife beating. Then, too, while leading questions are permitted and even encouraged on cross-examination, argumentative questions are not allowed. An American lawyer who asks a witness, "You're a liar, aren't you?" will soon find the judge sustaining an objection to this question by the opposing counsel.

Roman advocates, however, subjected the opposing side's witnesses to a tremendous amount of verbal abuse—with insulting questions and remarks about their appearance, behavior, and character. Cicero was famous for this. In one case, he allegedly told the court that it should completely ignore the fact that his opponent was an infamous philanderer who stole from innocent grandmothers!

In American courts today, cross-examination can be a very powerful weapon. It is well accepted by many lawyers that it is perfectly ethical to use cross-examination to impeach the credibility of a witness whom you know to be telling the truth. Indeed, a lawyer who would choose not to cross-examine an opposing witness because of respect for that witness's character or integrity would probably be in violation of the duty of zealous representation of the client.

For all this, however, cross-examination in American courts is nothing compared to the ruthless blackening of the name of the witness in which the skilled orators of the Roman courts would engage. One historian describes this process vividly: "Imagine yourself in court confronted by a Cicero in full cry: you would have to put up with a great deal of ritual abuse about your looks, habits, breeding, and so forth. For example, in [one case] . . . Cicero likened his client's opponent to a clown and alleged that he was ill-bred and a dabbler in fraudulent practices."[3]

Fear of this sort of cross-examination undoubtedly deterred many lawsuits. Several aspects of the procedural system of law in ancient Rome also put pressure on the parties to settle the case without going to trial. There are, of course, pressures on the litigants in modern American cases to settle, too. In criminal cases, we call this plea bargaining, and in civil cases settlement out of court is surely now more the norm than the exception. For years, American courts have also encouraged alternative dispute resolution, a term describing some ways of deciding cases without going to court.[4] But in ancient Rome, many other forces were at work encouraging settlement.

There was, for example, the matter of costs. In England and many civil countries today, litigation is discouraged by a rule that requires the losing party to pay the attorney fees of the winner as well as his own. But American courts tend not to adopt this rule, unless a statute specifically says otherwise. In America today, therefore, both parties normally pay their own attorney fees regardless of the trial's outcome, and attorney fees are usually the largest part of the cost of litigation.

Although advocates in republican Rome often did not take fees, both parties were often required to deposit a sum of money with the court as a wager on the trial's outcome. Only the winner of the case got the deposit back, and the fear of losing it helped contribute to the pressure to settle out of court.

Other factors encourage lawsuits in America and discouraged them in ancient Rome. In modern American law, the pretrial and trial stages of a case are governed by fairly detailed procedural rules in which the state plays an active role in seeing that there is a fair battle between the two parties and an exchange of information and evidence. In Rome, by contrast, the state's involvement in civil proceedings was at best minimal. For example, the state played very little if any role—at least in the law of republican and early imperial Rome—in ensuring that the defendant would show up for trial or in enforcing the judgment against the defendant. That was the plaintiff's job. A would-be plaintiff who was not confident that he would get his opponent into the courtroom or force him, by his own self-help, to pay the judgment assessed against him, would be hesitant to sue.

Then, too, many Romans apparently believed that there was often no point in suing because judges were frequently corrupt and susceptible to bribery. "The weak generally did not sue the strong," it is said, as they knew they would lose. A similarly cynical attitude prevails, of course, in the United States today. It is often said, for example, that the side with the more financial resources to hire not only lawyers but also expert witnesses and investigators will win the case.[5]

In ancient Rome, bringing a lawsuit against a powerful or popular person was likely to lead to ritual "shaming"—a practice whereby mobs of people congregated outside the home of an "offender" and taunted him with rude songs and verbal abuse. To avoid this kind of treatment, many citizens simply stayed out of court whenever possible.

But what if litigation was the only honorable course to pursue? How did procedure in the Roman courts differ from procedure in our own?

In American law, a civil case, of course, begins with the filing of a written complaint by the plaintiff, after which the defendant is served with process—informed of the lawsuit against him—and given an opportunity to answer the allegations in the complaint.

Under the *legis actiones* system, the early procedural system of Roman law, the plaintiff had to get the defendant into court by means of an oral summons—essentially a request that the defendant accompany the plaintiff to court. Nothing in court could be done without the consent of both parties; the plaintiff had to get the defendant to come. If the defendant refused to come, the plaintiff could use force to drag him there. But the state did not have to assist.

After what we would call these pleading stages, there was a preliminary hearing before a magistrate or praetor in which the issue before the parties would be determined. In our law, pleadings can be amended and are usually not rigidly bound by formal rules. In early Rome, as in most legal systems in their early stages, cases "began with a formal exchange of set words appropriate to the particular cause of action. A party could lose his claim through the slightest mistake at this stage."[6]

In our law, it is the plaintiff who chooses the forum—where the case is brought—initially. In Roman law, the action was usually only possible in the defendant's forum, although it is thought that the parties could agree on another location. In America, federal judges are appointed by the president while state judges are either elected, appointed, or selected by some compromise method. In republican Rome, judges were selected from an official list of senators who were empowered to decide cases. The magistrate who had presided at the preliminary hearing selected the judge.

The Roman trial also differed in important ways from our own. The modern American trial takes place indoors in a formal court setting; the Roman court was normally out of doors, often in the Forum Romanum, and, by contrast to the preliminary hearing, it was a fairly informal affair. In our courts, there are, of course, strict rules of evidence. Witnesses are compellable—that is, they can be forced to testify. In the Roman courts, under the *legis actiones*, there were few rules of evidence and witnesses were mostly not compellable. There was also no system of appeals in Roman republican law, unlike under our own law.

In modern American law, litigants can assume that the judgment will be enforced or executed with the full support of the state. Under the American Constitution, each state is even required to give "full faith and credit...to the public Acts, Records, and judicial Proceedings of every other state." This means, for example, that if I am successfully sued in Alabama, I cannot evade the judgment by escaping to New York. The courts of New York are obliged to enforce Alabama's judgment against me.

In Rome, by contrast, the state played a minimal role in execution of judgments. It was the plaintiff's job to see that the defendant paid up. The execution of the judgment was a sort of state-approved self-help.

This *legis actiones* system, however, was not to last forever. In time, as Rome expanded and grew more prosperous, Roman law grew more complex, and the flaws in the *legis actiones* system eventually made it seem inappropriate for litigation, much as changes in our economy and society have necessitated amendments to our Constitution. Actions at law were still confined to Roman citizens, but the praetor *peregrinus*—the praetor charged with the administration of justice concerning non-Roman citizens—developed a special procedure for cases involving foreigners. This procedure used formulae or simple written pleadings. Eventually, Roman citizens demanded that such a system be permitted for them.

The key to the formulary system was the plaintiff's presentation of a formula that typically had to be one of the standard ones allowed. In modern American law, the plaintiff's complaint must state the basis of the court's jurisdiction, the nature of the plaintiff's claim, and the remedy the plaintiff asks the court to bestow. Under the Roman formulary system, the formula had to name a judge (*nominatio*), state a claim (*intentio*), explain the facts from which the claim arose (*dem-*

onstratio), and state the requested remedy (*condemnatio*). A typical formula might run as follows: "Let Titus be judge. If it appears that the property which is disputed belongs to _____ at civil law, and if it be not restored to him...then you, judge, condemn _____ to _____ for so much of his property as the thing will be worth; if it does not appear, absolve him."[7]

There are some other interesting points of comparison between the formulary system and our law. American courts observe statutes of limitation, which set periods of time during which a person with a legal claim must bring an action or be precluded from doing so. There was, in ancient Rome, no equivalent of statutes of limitation for actions *ius civile* (at civil law). There was, however, an important equivalent of our injunctions: the remedy of the interdict instructed a person to do or refrain from doing something and was usually issued after a complaint by an aggrieved person.

The formulary system remained more or less dominant until well into the Roman imperial period. In time, it, too, gave way, as the magistrates, delegates of the emperor, became more and more the important players in the procedure of the law. As early as the reign of Augustus—the start, as we will soon see, of the Roman imperial period—we get the beginnings of a *cognitio* (investigation) procedure in which, as with our written complaint, it is a written statement of claim rather than an oral summons that begins the case. Unlike our common law trial, however, the *cognitio* trial procedure involved an investigation by the magistrate, who, far from being an umpire as in American common law courts, conducted the entire trial himself and made all the decisions. Such a court, of course, seems more like a modern civil law court, but it does bear some resemblance to our own common law courts. For one thing, cases were litigated in a courthouse rather than out in the open air. Parties also took an oath at the beginning of the trial, swearing to tell the truth. Witnesses could be subpoenaed to give evidence. Perhaps most important, a system of appeals developed along with a hierarchy of courts. The equivalent of the United States Supreme Court, in imperial Rome, was, of course,

the emperor, whose word was final in those cases in which he chose
to intervene.

Citizenship, Status, and Family Law

Under the Fourteenth Amendment to our Constitution, all persons
"born or naturalized in the United States and subject to the jurisdiction thereof are citizens of the United States and of the state wherein
they reside." Our law also speaks of persons, distinguishing between
natural persons and artificial persons like corporations.

Roman jurists generally meant human beings when they spoke
of "persons." Some entities were, however, treated as if they were
"persons" even if the law did not describe them that way. *Collegia*
were private clubs or societies that functioned as persons—like our
many associations that Tocqueville spoke so glowingly about. In the
Roman world, these *collegia* were usually dedicated to a particular
god.

The number of *collegia* rose rapidly in late republican Rome, and
the power of those associations was perceived as posing a danger to
public order, much as the growing number and resources of large corporations were seen by many as a threat to the commonweal in late-
nineteenth and early-twentieth-century America. We responded to
the threat from the growing corporations with antitrust laws. Rome
responded in other but similar ways. Julius Caesar limited the number of permitted *collegia*, and later Augustus prohibited the creation
of new *collegia* without consent of emperor and Senate.

Then there were *municipia* (from which, of course, our word
municipalities is derived), which, like our cities and towns, had various degrees of local autonomy and corporate character. There were
also charities in ancient Rome, and gifts to charities became more frequent after Emperor Constantine converted to Christianity. And, of
course, there was the legal entity called the state. The Roman people,
for example, could own things not capable of being privately owned.

The concept of publicly owned property is, of course, hardly unknown to American law as well.

As to the law of natural persons, status was all important for the Romans. In modern American property law, we speak of estates in land, and the word *estate* is derived from an old English word for *status*. In Roman law, there were three elements of status—*libertas* (freedom), *civitas* (citizenship), and *familia* (family). The man of full status possessed all three. He had *libertas* (he was free), *civitas* (he was a Roman citizen), and *familia* (he was a member of a Roman family).

Freedom (*libertas*) was the first criterion in defining the status of a Roman citizen. As Justinian's *Digest* later put it, "the great divide in the law of persons [in Rome] is this: all men are either free men or slaves" (1.5.3).[8] Freedom is there defined as "one's natural power of doing what one pleases, save insofar as it is ruled out either by coercion or by law" (*Digest* 1.5.4). Freedom, for the Romans, at least in their maturity, was thus perceived as the natural condition, slavery as unnatural. The same was true to a certain extent for the American Founding Fathers. A great student of Roman law and history although also a slave owner, Thomas Jefferson famously declared that "all men are created equal." While it tolerated slavery, the original American Constitution also prohibited the government from depriving a person of "life, liberty, or property without due process of law."

Whereas our law today confers citizenship by birth or naturalization, Roman law bestowed citizenship (*civitas*) automatically on a child if his mother was a citizen at the time of his birth. Citizenship could also be granted by the state as a reward for services rendered. Late in the Roman Empire, citizenship was extended to virtually all peoples throughout the Pax Romana.

Americans may carry a passport or social security card to prove their citizenship. Romans had a harder time proving it, but having three names (like Marcus Tullius Cicero) helped. The most definitive proof was provided by the Roman census, for which there is a clear modern-day American equivalent.

Citizens in the United States are, of course, guaranteed certain rights by the Constitution and by federal statutory law. Roman male citizens had three principal public law rights—the right to appeal against a death sentence, the right to vote in the *comitiae* (assemblies), and the right to run for office. Women had the right of appeal, but like women in many American states before 1920, they could not vote, and Roman women could not run for public office.[9] Private law rights included the *commercium,* or right to make contracts (our law asserts that those below the age of majority and the mentally incompetent lack capacity to enter binding contracts and can be released from the duty to perform); *testamenti facti,* or the right to make a valid will (we, too, speak of testamentary capacity as the capacity to write a valid will, and limit that capacity to persons who are "of sound mind"); and *conubium* (the right to make a civil law marriage).

Like most modern American matrimonial statutes, Roman law defined marriage as "the union of a man and a woman."[9] American law, of course, imposes a few restrictions on those who can marry. Both marrying individuals, first of all, must be of marrying age, which is generally sixteen or eighteen years in most American states. In Rome, women tended to marry very young, and ages of consent were generally twelve for females and fourteen for males.

In America today, a marriage license will not be granted if either of the parties is already married or there is a close blood relationship between them. In ancient Rome, as in American law, bigamy was outlawed and socially disapproved of as well. Marriages were also banned between persons related closely by blood. Lineal relatives could not marry—parent and child, grandparent and grandchild—nor could close collaterals: siblings could not marry, but cousins could.

Most important in Roman marriage law, as in American law: both parties had to have the capacity to consent at the time of the marriage. For the Romans, this meant that if either party was not *sui iuris* (legally independent),[10] he or she had to have the consent of the paterfamilias, or head of the household.

Our law really has no equivalent to the Roman paterfamilias. He was the oldest living male ancestor. He had the power of life and death over the children, including the right to expose newborn infants (the parents of Oedipus tried to have their child killed in this way in Sophocles's famous play),[11] the power to sell children into slavery, the right to refuse consent to marriage of children, and the right to compel them to marry.

The paterfamilias had no *potestas* (power) over an illegitimate child, and he could not expose or kill an illegitimate child although he could a legitimate one. In this respect, curiously, illegitimate children had more rights under Roman law than legitimate children.

What of parents who could not have children of their own? The English did not formally recognize adoption in law until the twentieth century.[12] The Romans had a well-developed adoption law by the late Republic and saw it as an important way to keep old families from becoming extinct.

Under the Twelve Tables, marriage between a patrician and a plebian was banned in early Rome. What were the Twelve Tables? Who were the patricians and the plebians? How did changes in laws like this reflect the growing democratization of Roman law? A brief survey of the constitutional development of Rome will shed light on our own legal and political evolution.

SIX

Roman Law from the Monarchy
to the Republic

A s Barry Nicholas of Oxford argues, "no system of law can be fully understood in isolation from the history of the society which it serves and regulates."[1] This is certainly true, of course, of the United States and our law. It is also true of Rome and Roman law. Moreover, studying the interrelation of law and society in Rome also means studying Roman political development.

When we studied ancient Greek history earlier, we saw that it fell into three main parts, roughly corresponding to the rise, golden age, and fall of this once-mighty city-state. In the history of ancient Rome's constitution, with an eye to the influence of Roman politics and especially Roman law on American constitutionalism, three similar periods or stages suggest themselves. The first brings Roman history from its origins down to about the year 146 BC, when Carthage was destroyed and Rome became a superpower even exceeding American hegemony today. In this first part belongs the Roman monarchy, the overthrow of the monarchy, the law of the Roman Republic, the rise of the plebian class, and the rise of Rome to world power. In much the same way, of course, the first period of American history chronicles the revolution against the British monarchy, the establishment of the American constitutional republic, the growing democratization of the Jeffersonian and Jacksonian eras, and the rise of American power. The second part of Roman constitutional history takes us through the decline and fall of the Roman Republic—through the age of Pompey and Julius Caesar, down to the principate of Augustus. The third period of Roman history begins with the principate and ends with the dominate; this is the era of the Pax Romana under a regime of absolute monarchy. The cycle had come full circle, 1,200 years later. It remains to be seen, of course, how much of the second and third periods of Roman history will be played out in the future story of the United States.

Monarchy: Early Constitutional History of Rome

In earliest Rome, the functions of the elective monarch (*rex*) have been described as "priest, general, and protector of domestic peace." Like the president of the United States, the king commanded the army in war. Like the Congress of the United States, the king could impose the taxes necessary to support a war. Unlike our president, the king was also the source of law and the head of the state religion. His power of life and death over the citizens, which could be exercised in time of war or, in time of peace, when their actions offended the state or the state religion, was symbolized by his purple robe and by the rods and axes (*fasces*) of his lectors. Later the Roman consuls would take over these ceremonial trappings of monarchy, just as our American presidency has adopted many of the ceremonial features of the English monarchy from which it was derived.

Also like our president, the Roman king was not a hereditary monarch. He was appointed by a Senate (just as our president, according to the original Constitution, is selected by an elite Electoral College) composed originally of heads of the clans (*gentes*, from which we derive our word *gentry*), who served as an advisory council to the king. The early Roman Senate had real power. If the king died, for example, the Senate governed the state until the next king took power. Later on in the Republic, if one of the consuls died, an interrex was appointed (an acting president?) and the period was called an interregnum.[2]

Our American Senate is, of course, an equal partner with the House of Representatives in the making of national law. It is important to note, however, that the Roman Senate had no legislative power as we know the term *legislative*, even in its mature phase during the Roman Republic. Its *senatus consulta* were highly prized and persuasive, but not binding as law (*lex*). We today still speak of the "advice and consent" of the Senate. The president of the United States must seek the "advice and consent of the Senate," for example, for ratification of treaties and appointment of justices of the Supreme Court and other "Officers of the United States."

There was also an assembly in early Rome called the comitia curiata in which each male citizen had one vote, but the whole assembly was divided into thirty curiae and it was the majority of curiae, not the majority of voters, that was counted. In much the same way, when the House of Representatives chooses our president in the event of a tie in the Electoral College, it is a majority of states, not a majority of representatives, that determines the outcome. The curiae of Rome, much like our states, were based on territorial and political divisions of all the citizens. The comitia curiata confirmed the Senate's choice of the king and officially conferred his power (*imperium*). This assembly, like the later Roman republican assemblies, met only when summoned by the presiding magistrate. Unlike our Congress, Roman assemblies could not initiate legislation; they only voted to approve or reject bills, not to discuss or amend them.

The role of the assembly in early Roman constitutional history was soon to change, however. During the reign of one of the last Roman kings, Servius Tullius, a new legislative assembly called the comitia centuriata emerged. When this assembly elected magistrates, passed laws, or declared war, the people voted by centuries. The richer citizens dominated the larger number of centuries and thus often controlled an essentially oligarchic legislative process.[3]

There are, of course, as we have seen, also unmistakable oligarchic features to our American Constitution. The popular description of the United States Senate as a "millionaires' club" is not without basis. It is well known that money plays a central role in American politics, and always has. For us, this fact is often a cause for embarrassment. But like Aristotle, the Romans understood that these oligarchic features can be a source of strength. The mixed constitution that the Romans eventually developed, as the Greek historian of Rome Polybius tells us, brought together democratic and oligarchic features and checked and balanced power, much as our American Constitution does.

But we are not yet at the stage of Rome's republican constitution. In retrospect, we can see that Rome benefited greatly from her seven kings. During their reign, the city expanded and came to dominate a large party of Italy. In later republican days, it became fashionable to castigate the monarchy and remember these early days with scorn, in much the same way that it is often fashionable in American schools today to condemn our Founding Fathers as wealthy, racist, and insensitive. But the Roman kings, like the American framers, laid the foundations for future greatness.

In time, that early Roman kingship hardened into a tyranny. The seventh and final king, Tarquin the Proud, reduced the Senate to insignificance and appealed over the heads of the senators (and thus over the heads of the nobility) to the people. American presidents appeal over the heads of our senators to the people, too. They do it with weekly radio addresses—modern-day "fireside chats"—and occasional press conferences. But presidents also have enemies in the press, and Tarquin the Proud had similar enemies in his day. An anti-monarchist propagandist named Junius Brutus started to tell people that the king's family was riddled with corruption and immorality. In time, the Romans acted. Nobody wants to obey a corrupt and immoral king. The kings were expelled—a more final remedy than our impeachment. A chapter in the history of the Roman constitution had come to an end.

The Rise of the Roman Republican Constitution

The expulsion of the kings in 509 BC was the first major change in the constitutional history of Rome—much as the Constitutional Convention of 1787 gave us the first major change in our legal development. From 509 BC on, a Roman republican constitution began to take shape. The king was replaced by two magistrates called consuls, who were endowed with full executive power (*imperium*), held office for only a year, and were each subject to the veto of the other.

There are many grounds for comparison of the Roman consuls and the American president. When one considers what Hamilton said in *The Federalist Papers* about the need for a single executive, one senses how much had been learned about the dangers of having two heads of state:

> Energy in the executive is a leading character in the definition of good government.... The ingredients which constitute energy in the executive are unity; duration; an adequate provision for its support; and competent powers.... That unity is conducive to energy will not be disputed. Decision, activity, secrecy, and dispatch will generally characterize the proceedings of one man in a much more eminent degree than the proceedings of any greater number; and in proportion as the number is increased, these qualities will be diminished. This unity may be destroyed...by vesting the power in two or more magistrates of equal dignity and authority.... The two consuls of Rome may serve as an example.... The Roman history records many instances of mischiefs to the republic from the dissensions between the consuls.[4]

Like our presidency today, throughout the history of the Roman Republic, the office of consul was the highest political prize. Much like our president, the consul received ambassadors and transmitted all foreign correspondence as well as messages from generals in the field to the Senate. In time of war, the consuls were commanders in chief, and they often served in the field themselves, at the head of their troops.

To the Roman people, especially in the early days of the Republic, the consuls must have seemed to control the state. They wore a distinctive toga with a broad purple band and scarlet shoes and they had an escort of twelve lectors, each bearing the symbol of the state's power—the fasces, or a bundle of rods, bound together around two axes. Much later, of course, the term *fascist* was derived from this, and this image has also been engraved on American coins. American presidents also have their royal rituals. They are, for example, inaugurated in an impressive monarchial ritual complete with parades, triumphant music, and, most important, the swearing of a great oath, which is similar in important ways to the coronation oath of the English kings.

The Roman consuls were a force to be reckoned with. Understandably, the Romans often counted dates not by the year after the founding of the city, but by the name of the consul who was in office at the time. As Polybius said, "men do not rashly resist the powers of the consuls."[5]

Still, there were important limits on the consuls' powers, just as there are limits on the president's powers today. With his veto, each consul could stop the other from taking any actions of which he did not approve. In time of war, this meant that one consul was in command of the army one day and the other consul was in command the next.[6] Although they were supreme in the field, the consuls depended on the Senate to raise armies and pay for the expenses of war, just as our president is dependent on Congress to provide the funds for military operations that he orders. As Polybius wrote, "without a decree of the Senate, [troops] can be supplied neither with corn nor clothes nor pay, so that all the plans of a commander must be futile if the Senate is resolved either to shrink from danger or hamper his plans."[7] Woodrow Wilson found this out when the United States Senate refused to approve his cherished League of Nations. Other American presidents have faced impeachment when their popularity waned. And the Romans had an institution like impeachment for the consuls as well. If the people did not like a consul, he could be forced to abdicate and then tried by the Senate.

In the early years of the Republic, practically all of the executive power of Rome was concentrated in the consuls—in much the same way as the "executive power shall be vested in a President of the United States" in the opening words of Article II of our American Constitution. Over the next century, however, the business of the consuls grew so much that it became necessary to give them helpers and assistants. Our presidents, of course, also came to need more and more help as well, but the bureaucracy at the federal level in America is fundamentally hierarchical. At the top of the pyramid, the president can appoint and—as Andrew Jackson first taught us by practical example—remove the heads of the various departments. But that was not true in republican Rome. These lesser magistrates were not chosen by the consuls. They were elected independently, and could not be dismissed by the consuls. They thereby gained a measure of independence and authority.

First, two quaestores were assigned to examine the public accounts and supervise public administration. Later, around 443 BC, the office of censor was created. The censors looked into how many citizens there were and how much property they owned. We take our modern "census" every ten years. The Romans took theirs every five years, and the process of counting took about eighteen months, which was just the term of office of the censors.

More significantly, the censors came to have the power to place a mark (*nota*) against the name of any man whose behavior they condemned. This stigma resulted in practical disenfranchisement, and was part of the censors' general supervisory authority over morality. Even today, we use the term censured for a reprimand or rebuke. A president can be censured—a mark of disapproval short of impeachment. Andrew Jackson was censured by the Senate when he fired his secretary of the Treasury.

Still later, about 367 BC, a praetor was first appointed to help the consuls with the growing business of the law courts. From that date on, the consuls no longer presided in the law courts, and the praetor who did preside, called the praetor *urbanus*, or city praetor, had assistant judges who were in charge of the actual trials. We, too, have magistrates as a kind of assistant judge in our system of courts.

Parties to cases that were about to come to trial naturally wanted to know what the law was and how it was going to be applied. In time, it thus became customary for the praetor *urbanus*, every year on his assumption of office, to make a public statement of the law he would apply. This public statement was his *edictum* (from this we derive our term *edict*) and comprised the instructions (*formulae*) that he intended to give to his judges. Eventually the praetors, who became the chief administrators of the Roman legal system, like modern ministers of justice, issued these edicts on wax tablets that were displayed in the Forum at the start of the praetor's term of office. In time, most of the edict was comprised of rules adopted from the previous praetor. Over time, the custom of relying on past decisions of previous praetors became entrenched, and therein we see the origins of stare decisis, or precedent, which, of course, is at the heart of our common law.

For the Romans, a consistent set of rules was thus passed on from one year to the next, and this contributed to the development of what came to be called the *ius honorarium*—"the law of those in honorary positions." This became an important supplement to the civil law (*ius civile*) for Roman citizens, much as equity later supplemented English common law. But what if one party to the case was a foreigner or a noncitizen?

In our Constitution, Congress is given the power to confer on the federal courts "foreign diversity" jurisdiction to hear cases between citizens of the United States and citizens or subjects of a foreign state. Congress has, of course, conferred such jurisdiction on the federal district courts, along with domestic diversity jurisdiction to hear cases brought between citizens of different American states.

In 242 BC in Rome, the potential for cases involving foreigners meant that another office had to be created, that of praetor *peregrinus*, or foreign praetor, who was charged with looking after such cases. The law governing the rights of foreigners and noncitizens came to be called the *ius gentium*, or law of other peoples.

In sum, then, this growing power of the praetors, along with the rise in the power of other magistrates such as the censors, began to change the constitutional stature of the consuls and effect a change in the whole constitution of the Republic. The biggest constitutional changes of the republican era, however, can be attributed to the class cleavage in Roman society between the patricians and the plebians, in much the same way that the most important changes in the American Constitution, at least since the Civil War, must be understood in light of the growing democratization of American society.

When the kings had ruled Rome, the patrician nobles had been kept under control. After the monarchy ended, however, the nobles acquired more and more power over the plebians. By about 500 BC, these plebians started demanding some power to control the arbitrary magistrates, just as American farmers and urban workers began to demand more power in the Populist and Progressive movements near the start of the twentieth century. In time, the Roman plebians were granted their own assembly (*concilium plebis*), which would elect tribunes and would legislate (plebiscite) in matters that concerned only the plebians.

More demands followed—in particular, that the law be written down, much as the poor of Athens had demanded written law in the days before Draco's first *Code of Laws*. A body of ten men (*decemvirs*) was appointed to codify the existing law. They were granted extraordinary power; indeed the whole machinery of government came to an end while they held office, just as the whole machinery of the Articles of Confederation effectively came to an end as the Convention met in Philadelphia in the summer of 1787 to draft the Constitution of the United States.

These *decemvirs* issued a code of laws on ten (possibly wooden) tablets. These laws were thought by many to be incomplete, so a second group of *decemvirs*, this time with some plebians included, wrote two more tablets of laws. This code was acknowledged from the outset as a basic statement of the law of Rome. It came to be known as the Twelve Tables, the first truly important document of Roman law.

British historian Frank Cowell tells us that the "Romans may have thought about the Twelve Tables rather as the average Englishman or American, untrained in medieval constitutional law and practice, has regarded Magna Carta, as a respectable historical guarantee which he could invoke to justify his own desires and political ambitions.... Yet the Twelve Tables were generally referred to by Roman writers as the first complete statement of the whole body of Roman law, public, criminal, and private."[8]

There is a great deal of legal detail and even, one might say, sophistication in the Twelve Tables. For instance, there were provisions for capital punishment for traitors—treason is still the only crime mentioned and defined in the United States Constitution—and penalties for judges who took bribes. The ancient right of a citizen to appeal to the assembly (*comitia centuriata*) was affirmed, just as the ancient writ of habeas corpus was affirmed in our Constitution.

Roman legal historian Hans Julius Wolff says that, for "a thousand years, the XII Tables remained the only attempt ever made by the Romans at a comprehensive codification of their laws."[9] As such, the Tables were revered by subsequent generations. Cicero later said he learned them by heart as a young schoolboy, in much the same way that American schoolchildren used to memorize the Preamble of our Constitution. The Roman historian Livy called them "the fount of all Roman law, public and private."

The Twelve Tables did much to mollify plebian dissatisfaction, but not enough. Their unrest continued to rise. A new chapter in the history of Rome's constitution was in the making.

SEVEN

The Republic in Decline and the Empire

The early constitutional history of Rome is the story of the formation of a powerful common will. Every state faces a similar problem—how to get all the people, collectively, to want and will what the nation as a whole must do. Lincoln faced that problem in our Civil War, and solved it with the victorious armies of Generals Grant and Sherman.

In antiquity, before Rome could achieve this common will, she had to go through a devolution of power—from the rule of one (the king), to the rule of few (the patrician aristocracy), to the rule of many (the gradual leveling up of the plebians to fitness to rule). Our nation has gone through a comparable devolution—from rule by a king (George III), to rule by an aristocracy (the Founding Fathers), to a gradually democratized rule in modern times.

The Romans recorded every stage of this devolution of power, and of the class struggle between patrician and plebian, in their public law, or *ius civile*. As the Roman Republic evolved, the *ius civile* changed, as strikes by the plebians forced the patricians to make a series of concessions, resulting in changes in the constitution. We have already mentioned the first such change: the plebians were given the right to elect tribunes. Later, by the Lex Canuleia of 445 BC, intermarriage between patricians and plebians was permitted. By 367, the consulship was opened to plebians. By 340 BC, one of the two consuls had to be a plebian. In much the same way, our American Constitution was gradually democratized, as we saw, first in the Jeffersonian era with the Bill of Rights, then in the Jacksonian era with the elimination of most property qualifications for voting and holding office, and then in the post–Civil War and Progressive eras with the amendments guaranteeing the right to vote regardless of race or gender and forbidding states to deny due process or equal protection of the law. Through all this time, Rome was consolidating by war its control of what is now called the Italian peninsula and setting up an ancient equivalent of our Monroe Doctrine: no peace was negotiated with enemies that stood on Italian soil. In much the same way, of course, America consolidated its control of the North American continent, through wars on the frontier and a war with Mexico, in the nineteenth century.

Then, around 267 BC, in a momentous move—a move that has been compared by the great classical historian Eduard Meyer to the decision of the United States to go to war with Spain in 1898—Rome for the first time decided to cross the straits of Messina separating Rome and Sicily and take an interest in territory beyond the limits of the Italian peninsula. Thus began the Punic Wars with Carthage.

It was in the Second Punic War that Carthage, under the command of the brilliant general Hannibal—who has sometimes been compared to the great Confederate general Robert E. Lee—invaded Italy by crossing through the French and Swiss Alps on elephants, and defeated the Romans at the battle of Cannae at the gates of Rome. The Greek historian of Rome Polybius—the man who taught the Romans how to write history—asks how it is that, in only fifty-three years after the disastrous defeat at Cannae, Rome was able not only to defeat Carthage but also to make itself master of the known world. Polybius's answer is that Rome's mixed constitution of checks and balances, an antecedent of our own Constitution of checks and balances, is chiefly responsible.

Polybius understood that those checks and balances permitted the plebians to compete with the patricians without destroying the state. It was precisely because of that competition, not because of cooperation, that Rome conquered. The patricians and plebians would not cooperate even to defeat the enemy. They competed with each other to defeat the enemy. The force of that competition was so passionate, so strong, that the result was a victory of unprecedented magnitude.[1] Polybius explains the impact of that victory on the world:

> Previously the doings of the world had been, so to say, dispersed, as they were held together by no unity of initiative, results or locality; but...[now] history has become an organic whole and the affairs of Italy and Libya have been interlinked with those of Greece and Asia, all leading to one end....For it was owing to their defeat of the Carthaginians in the Hannibalic War that the Romans...were first emboldened to reach out their hands to...cross with an army to Greece and the continent of Asia.[2]

Hardened in their foreign policy attitude by demagogues like Cato the Elder, Rome finally, in the Third Punic War, totally destroyed Carthage and the city site was cursed. From then on, the Roman Empire was born and the Roman Republic, doomed.

A great powerful force is released when a multiplicity of wills that have been working at cross-purposes come to work together toward one end. That is what happened to America after our Civil War. And it is what happened to Rome in the Punic Wars. All the pent-up force of the patrician/plebian antagonism got directed against the external enemy. And that is how, as Polybius notes, in less than fifty-three years, Rome went from the total defeat of Cannae to Rome's total destruction of Carthage in 146 BC.

Rome then suddenly found itself in a situation much like that of the United States after the Cold War.

It suddenly became, as we did in our time, the world's only superpower.

Polybius had predicted that, in her new role Rome would experience chaos and civil war and eventually turn to despotism. Several hundred years later, Saint Augustine would rightly say that Rome's destruction of Carthage was the start of Rome's long decline. As

Henry Paolucci describes it, "the fall of the Empire was merely a five hundred year delay in the ultimate collapse of the Republic."[3]

After the destruction of Carthage—a destruction, it has been said, far surpassing the American leveling of Hiroshima and Nagasaki in Japan in 1945—the Roman Republic, deprived of its only external enemy, began to turn in on itself with the savagery of class warfare. One wonders whether America, too, might have, in time, fallen prey to such internal conflict, after the end of the Cold War, had not the challenge of a war against terrorists given some impetus to unity.

Just like Athens after the death of Pericles, Rome fell to the mob. The great historian of Rome Theodor Mommsen gives us a vivid explanation of the kinds of demands that were made: "The rabble began to demand as its right that the future consul should recognize and honor the sovereign people in every ragged idler of the street, and that every candidate should, in his 'going round,' salute every individual voter by name and press his hand.... The candidate...recommended himself to the multitude by flattering attentions, indulgences, and civilities."[4]

One after another, Roman politicians came forward, proposing to act for Rome in the name of justice. The FDR of Republican Rome, Tiberius Gracchus, was a noble who tried to be a benefactor of the common people against all other classes. Tiberius and his brother were assassinated, however, much as John and Robert Kennedy were assassinated in the 1960s when they tried to champion the cause of the common man. The philosopher Hegel describes the civil war that followed in Rome: "The Roman state...came to be rent asunder by quarrels about dividing the spoils. Ruin now broke in unchecked, and, as there existed no generally recognized and absolutely essential object to which the country's energy could be devoted, individualities and physical force were in the ascendant."[5]

In the late Republic, men came to power in Rome by becoming masters of the army. First there was Marius. Then came his young aide Sulla.

Like Machiavelli centuries later, Sulla has not been treated kindly by historians. Historian Mommsen explains that he called things by their right name with brutal frankness. Thus he has irreparably offended the great mass of the weak-hearted who are more offended at the name than at the thing.[6]

Constitutionally, Sulla tried to restore the power of the Roman aristocracy. His constitutional reforms were a last attempt to save the checks and balances of the mixed republican constitution that Polybius had said was the key to Rome's republican greatness. But as soon as Sulla laid down his power, his system fell apart. In the succeeding scramble, Pompey ultimately won only when he totally repudiated Sulla's constitution.

Sulla had said that a great leader had to listen to the Senate. Pompey listened. And while he was listening, another great general acted. His name was, of course, Julius Caesar.

Once he had gained a monopoly of force, Caesar set out to give Rome a universal Pax Romana—an enforceable peace of Roman law and order. The leading republicans of Caesar's day, however, led by Brutus and Cassius, determined that, while such a concentration of power might be needed to enforce universal peace, it might also greatly endanger the liberties of Romans. Caesar, to them, might appear to be a republican—rejecting the crown not once but thrice in Shakespeare's play—though in reality he was a threat to the Roman constitution and rule of law.

How much does freedom matter? That is the central question of our own time. In ancient Roman times, these early republican diehards concluded that freedom mattered enough to turn them into assassins—assassins who, by their deed, unwittingly plunged Rome into an even darker cycle of civil war and chaos from which it emerged only with the complete and utter despotism of Julius Caesar's nephew Octavian, known to history as Augustus.

Augustus adopted a kind of legal fiction. In other words, he changed the constitution drastically without appearing to change it much at all. The magistrates, for example, were to be elected in the same way as before, but in practice no magistrate who did not have the approval of Augustus would dare even run for office.

The Senate and assemblies still met and went about their business, but that business was in reality confined to confirming—and never disputing—what Augustus (the emperor) said. In theory, the emperor was only—like our poor vice president—*princeps senatus*, or president of the Senate. The emperor's power was unobtrusive; he respected scrupulously all the legal formalities. In reality, however, he had all the consuls' military power, including supreme command of the army—like our American president—as well as the right to introduce all legislation and veto all legislation.

The Roman historian Tacitus gives, in one memorable sentence, a summary of the achievement of Augustus: "Augustus won over the soldiers with gifts, the populace with cheap grain,...and so grew greater by degrees, while he concentrated in himself the functions of the Senate, the magistrates, and the laws."[7]

The republican Tacitus also says that the Romans accepted Augustus because they did not want to turn back to the bloodshed of the Republic. They "preferred the safety of the present to the dangerous past." Another Roman historian, Sallust, tells us that, before the destruction of Carthage, the ultimate coercive power in Rome had been the external enemy. When that enemy was gone, the Romans came eventually to learn that only absolute rule could hold the Roman people together.

Roman Constitutional Law under the Empire

The Romans had assassinated Julius Caesar because they thought he was trying to do something unnecessary and dangerous—to make himself dictator. In time, they came to realize that, in the post-Carthage world, a dictator was a necessity. Henry Paolucci explains the predicament: "The second time around, Augustus asked: 'Have you learned yet?' This time he got the people's consent. The Romans had killed Caesar but accepted Augustus. Although in later years they were to kill many unsuitable emperors, it never crossed their minds to restore the republic. What was the republic but six armies trying to kill each other?"⁸ In other words, the Romans had come to appreciate that they had to create an internal domestic equivalent of the enemy's external force, to hold themselves together.

Augustus used his powers wisely, giving the impression—again, much as Lincoln would do during our Civil War—that he was acting constitutionally. The constitutional result was a new mix of the traditional forms of the Republic, but under the rule of a *princeps*, or first citizen. In the years after Augustus, the republican institutions gradually lost all semblance of power. The Senate became a body of yes-men. Only the army as an institution remained important, for emperors needed the support of the army.

This absolutism begun by Augustus is best expressed in the Corpus Juris of Justinian. It is in this *Corpus Juris*—and particularly in the *Institutes*—that we find the two great maxims of Roman imperial rule. The first is *quod principi placuit legis habet vigorem* (whatever pleases the prince has the force of law). But how is this absolutism of the prince made legal? The people, by the *Lex Regia*, make over to him their whole power and authority, Justinian says. *Princeps legibus solutus* is the second maxim. The prince is not under the law. He is the source of law.

None of this can be taken as a general legal principle, applicable to all times. This is absolutism pure and simple, and absolutism is essential only for a people with no external enemy. The maxims of absolutism are in some ways like the absolute power that an American Lincoln or Roosevelt exercises when the nation is threatened in time of war. But unlike the Roman absolutism, the American president's prerogative is deliberately left vague and undefined in the Constitution. With no external enemy and the threat of endless civil war staring them in the face, the Romans could not afford to be so vague. They are the only people in the history of the world who truly made themselves the masters with no external enemies and then could not conceal the absolutism to which they had to resort in order to save themselves from anarchy.

With Justinian, we are at the end of the constitutional history of ancient Rome. The western empire was being swallowed up by marauding tribes from the north. A new chapter in the history of constitutionalism—a chapter with even greater significance for American law—was about to begin.

PART THREE

The English Constitution and English Common Law

EIGHT

The Importance and Origins
of the English Constitution

The ancient Greeks gave America and the West a humanist orientation, love of freedom, and the rule of law. The ancient Romans gave us the science of law and natural law. It was England, however, that gave America the common law and the system of representative constitutional government. One of the most remarkable and successful political organizations the world has known, this system strikes a balance between individual self-determination and governmental power that makes possible an ordered civilized "government by discussion."[1]

It is not the balance that the ancient world struck. The classical Athenians and republican Romans of antiquity would have despised representative government because freedom was only possible if all the citizens could make the laws themselves. Praising this city-state ideal of pure democracy many centuries later in France, Jean-Jacques Rousseau would say the English were only free on election day. The ancient Greeks and Romans would have said that about us. Only on election day do we make any political choices for ourselves. On all other days, we are ruled by others, even if we call them our "representatives."

It was the English who changed this. Thomas Hobbes—who wrote around 1650, after the constitutional system had been molded by centuries of English kings and parliaments—is the first great philosopher to give the world a well-developed modern theory of representative government. In *Leviathan*, Hobbes explains how "a multitude of men are made one person, when they are by one man, or one person, represented." He says the object of the social contract is "to appoint one man, or assembly of men, to bear their person; and every one to own, and acknowledge himself to be author of whatsoever he that so beareth their person, shall act or cause to be acted."[2]

From his theory of representative government can be traced the constitutional monarchy theory of John Locke and the representative republic envisioned by our Founding Fathers. It would be a cardinal error to assume that Hobbes *invented* representative government, however. The reality emerged far earlier in history than its theoretical exposition.

The greatest historian of English law, Frederick William Maitland, says in his *Constitutional History of England* that "the notion of the representation of the community by some of its members must have been old." In time, you see the emergence of a Parliament of three estates, "clergy, barons, and commons, those who pray, those who fight, and those who work," which develops into "an assembly of the estates of the realm."[3] In the colonies, a colonial legislature becomes heir of this representative tradition. At the national level in America, we get first the two Continental Congresses, then the Congress of the Articles of Confederation, and finally the Congress of the Constitution. Representative government through popularly elected assembly becomes one of England's greatest contributions to American constitutionalism.

The other great English contribution, of course, is the common law. It is today quite customary to speak of the United States, like Britain, as a common law country. To the modern lawyer, this means that most of our law is judge-made, and that statutes must be understood against a wide backdrop of law evolved through precedent. This is not the original meaning of the term *common law*, however. In his *Constitutional History*, Maitland gives a capsule summary of the term that first comes into use around the time of Edward I (reigned 1272–1307):

The word "common" of course is not opposed to "uncommon"; rather it means "general."...Common law is in the first place unenacted law; thus it is distinguished from statutes and ordinances. In the second place, it is common to the whole land; thus, it is distinguished from local customs. In the third place, it is the law of the temporal courts; thus, it is distinguished from ecclesiastical law....More common law is gradually evolved as ever new cases arise; but the judges are not conceived as making new law—they have no right or power to do that—rather they are but declaring what has always been law.[4]

In today's American law schools, the first-year common law subjects are contracts, torts, and property. The English common law tradition is also vital, however, in understanding American *constitutional* law. James Stoner makes this point in his book *Common Law Liberty:* "The American Constitution and American constitutional law cannot be understood without reference to the common-law tradition in which they were formed.... [Moreover,] the common law is a key to understanding the fundamental principles of our Constitution and a guide for deciding contemporary constitutional cases."[5]

Stoner goes on to cite clauses in the original Constitution and the Bill of Rights that can only be interpreted in light of English common law precedents and principles—phrases like *habeas corpus, ex post facto, bill of attainder,* and *trial by jury.* In sum, Stoner writes, our whole common law system "would be recognizable to a seventeenth-century Englishman: the mixed regime of judge and jury in the courtroom, adversarial proceedings, a bench drawn from the bar, the legal force accorded precedent, the way first principles of government appear in the context of particular cases, the importance of individual rights and government by law." As Norman Cantor puts it in his book *Imagining the Law: Common Law and the Foundations of the American Legal System,* "the constitutional and political significance of the English common law heritage has been an enduring if complex theme in American history."[6]

Together, a system of representative government and the common law are two vital influences of the English constitution on American law. That English constitution, however, did not spring up suddenly, fully formed, as it were, out of the mind of Zeus. It evolved and developed, gradually, over centuries. To understand the English constitution and its relevance to America, it is essential to know about its historical evolution.

While it is difficult to appreciate the contemporary American or French constitutions, for example, without knowing something of American or French history, it is utterly impossible to appreciate the English constitution without a knowledge of English constitutional history. Like the ancient Romans and unlike the Americans and the French and most other peoples of the modern world, the English do not have a written constitution. Their "constitution" *is* the history. It is this series of traditions and accumulated precedents, both parliamentary and judicial, that has shaped and formed English law. This constitution has been flexible enough to withstand and adapt to convulsions as dramatic as the Norman Conquest and the Reformation.

Moreover, as Cantor notes, there "is a close connection . . . between the common law and English liberal political institutions"; it is impossible to study the evolution of English common law and its lessons for America without referring to the evolution of the English monarchy and of Parliament. A careful historical review of the long development of the English constitution and English constitutional institutions from England's earliest days up to the colonization and founding of America can thus do much to illuminate the American constitutional tradition that it so greatly influenced.

Roman Law in Roman Britain

Law on the North American continent is often said to begin with the first European settlers. Similarly, law on the island of Britain can first be seen through the eyes of the conquering Romans.

In 55 BC, trying to stabilize Gaul, Julius Caesar decided to make a show of strength north of what is today the English Channel. With an army of five legions, he crossed the waters that centuries later would hold back Napoleon and Hitler and defeated the natives on the banks of the river Thames—the river which, as he wrote, "can be forded only at one place and that with difficulty."

Caesar's diaries describe the native priest-judges, called Druids, who enforced and maintained the Celtic laws—more precisely customs and religion—for the Britons whom his armies overwhelmed. Law in the beginning, unlike our law, is nearly always primarily oral—characterized by custom and oaths, not by written codes. This was true of archaic Greek law. It was also certainly true of the law—if we can call it law—of the Celtic peoples on the island of Britain before Julius Caesar came.

Caesar actually tells us very little about the specifics of the Celtic legal customs he encountered in the natives he conquered, except that they involved human sacrifices. Perhaps this is because, as one contemporary legal historian puts it, the "Romans themselves had a sophisticated jurisprudence, and to them the usages of the British had little more than anthropological interest."[7]

Caesar's visit, really an armed reconnaissance aimed at discouraging British tribes from assisting their kindred in Gaul, was only the first chapter in the story of the law of Roman Britain. In AD 43, almost a hundred years after Caesar's assassination, the Romans sent an army of forty thousand under Emperor Claudius. Once again, the natives were subdued. The Romans built a bridge and established a settlement. In a decade, Londinium was a growing city where Roman law flourished.

In *Imagining the Law*, Cantor reminds us that the Roman imperial law then flourishing in Londinium put a premium on rationalization, order, and uniformity. There have been attempts at rationalization and simplification of law in America, too. A codification of federal commercial law, begun in the 1950s, for example, resulted in the miracle that we now know as "the Uniform Commercial Code."

On the whole, however, Cantor says, total codification "is improbable in Anglo-American law because...there are too many vested interests enjoying benefits from the current infinite and inefficient legal corpus."[8] We have never had a comprehensive statutory reworking of our law of property, contract, and tort, and we probably never will.

A similar problem beset the Romans trying to rationalize and coordinate law in Britain. It is true that, from Londinium, the Roman governor Agricola (AD 77–84) sought to extend the Roman system of law courts throughout what is now the entire island of Britain. But in all the 350 years they remained on the island, the Romans never managed to complete Agricola's goals and turn all of Britain into a Roman province under Roman law.

Protected by its walls, Londinium itself became thoroughly Roman in law and culture. Outside the city walls, however, Britain was never fully absorbed into this Roman world. Half the people living on the island had almost no contact with Roman law. Tribes continued to live in stone huts—as removed from the Romanized Londoners in their villas as they were close in spirit to the Celtic tribes in Gaul. Such tribesmen only came in contact with Roman law through soldiers, bureaucrats, and tax collectors. They resented Roman authority, and when other barbarian tribes from the North began breaching Hadrian's Wall and penetrating the South, these local tribes joined them in raids on Londinium and the other Roman settlements of the South.

"The decline was rapid." As Sir Frederick Pollock and Frederick William Maitland remind us in their masterful *History of English Law*, "the Roman armies were becoming barbarous hosts." By 407, the Romans had abandoned Britain, and the collapse of the whole empire was not far off. "Indeed," Pollock and Maitland add, "the fall of a loose stone in Britain brought the whole crumbling edifice to the ground."[9] The Roman legions were gone. A thick fog descended over the city of London. Tribes of Angles and Saxons moved in. With no use for Roman law, they turned London into a ghost town. So it remained for nearly two hundred years.

Anglo-Saxon England and the Origins of the English Constitution

The Angles, Saxons, and Jutes were barbaric Teutonic tribes of tall, fair-haired people from northern Europe. Beginning in the fifth century, they poured into eastern England, moving west up the rivers and along the old Roman roads, sacking and burning as they went.

After centuries of conquest and assimilation, we get a revival of law. Around 600, Pope Gregory the Great sent Augustine to England to Christianize the natives. With Christianity came literacy, and with literacy came law. In the seventh century, King Ethelbert of Kent, the first English Christian monarch, gave us what the historian Maitland calls "the first English laws that were ever put into writing."[10] Ethelbert was a contemporary of the Roman emperor Justinian, whose *Corpus Juris* "developed the legal culture that predated by half a millennium...English common law."[11] Maitland elaborates on the coincidence of the dates of Justinian at the end of the first life of Roman law and Ethelbert at the start of English law: "Thus the history of English law may be said to begin just about the time when the history of Roman law—we will not say comes to an end, for in a certain sense it has never come to an end—but comes to a well-marked period."[12]

Ethelbert's "laws" were, as the Venerable Bede said, written "in the Roman style" but in the "English" language—or, more precisely, in the Anglo-Saxon vernacular. Pollock and Maitland call them "the first Germanic laws that were written in the Germanic tongue."[13] On the continent, Maitland adds, Latin continued to be the language of the law for centuries. "But our earliest laws are written in English,...and until the Norman Conquest all [English] laws were written in English."[14]

Like Justinian and unlike American legislators, King Ethelbert did not really *make* laws at all. His laws are a compilation of the customs of his day—a mirror of the rigidly hierarchical society in which each person's worth was determined by his *wergild*—a sum of money that had to be paid as compensation to the lord of a murdered man. The legal world of Ethelbert was not, like ours, a world of courts and judges, however. It was a world of blood feuds and localized justice. There was no England, no king of England. The Germanic tribes who had conquered had known little central authority and no kings. But soon, kingdoms began to take shape on the island that would later be England—Northumbria in the North, Mercia in the midlands, and Wessex in the South. In time, just as in the early development of the kingships of Athens and Rome, each king came to rely on an assembly of the wise for advice. Gradually, the powers of this assembly, or *witan*, an early ancestor of our Congress, grew. When eventually the kingdoms would merge into one kingdom of England, the *witan* would become what Maitland calls the first nationwide English assembly.

In the years after Ethelbert, the situation was like what our sovereign states faced under the Articles of Confederation and what the ancient Greek city-states experienced before their forced unification by Alexander the Great. Like those ancient Greek city-states, the Anglo-Saxon kingdoms soon fell prey to another round of invaders—the Vikings. These Norsemen were, as William McElwee notes, "in almost all respects what the Saxons themselves had been 400 years before, but writ large"[15]—fair-haired pirates who came in long ships that eventually "colonized" Greenland and "discovered" North America.

The central figure of this chapter in the history of English law is Alfred the Great, whom historian Christopher Hibbert calls "the first great statesman to emerge from the mists of early English history."[16] Alfred is "the king who saved England against seemingly hopeless odds."[17] In the peace he gained by conquest and treaty, he legislated for a united English people, promulgating "the first English laws to be consciously enacted."[18] When Alfred died, England was united as never before. His successors did what they could to preserve his legacy of uniformity through law. The idea of the "king's peace," which it was the king's sworn duty to protect and maintain, began to emerge. The legal authority of the monarch spread further and more deeply in England than it had in any other European country of that time.

Kings began to promulgate more detailed law codes called dooms. Cantor describes these as "relatively short documents, usually written in Old English." The "greater part of the law remained oral and never written down. It was retained in the memory of the older magnates...who were therefore called 'doomsmen.'"[19]

The Anglo-Saxon dooms give us what Maitland calls "a continuous series of laws" from Alfred the Great down to the last Anglo-Saxon king, Edward the Confessor, (reigned 1042–1065), who became so committed to the building of his great abbey—the forerunner of the present-day Westminster Abbey on what was then a desolate island in the Tyburn River—that he moved his royal residence, and that of his council, to be near it.

This decision was of enormous constitutional and political significance. It started the development of a center of royal and legal power at Westminster. In time, this led to the separation between the financial city of London and the political capital at Westminster—a separation that would influence much of English and therefore American legal history. Isolated from the commercial center, English law was free to develop.

As to how it began to develop, we have, perhaps surprisingly, little direct evidence. As Maitland describes, the legal literature of this period is scanty—no treatises of law and "very few accounts of litigation." There is, as yet, no "common law," because "the phrase implies law common to the whole kingdom, and how much law there was common to the whole kingdom in the days before the Norman Conquest is a very difficult question."[20] Still, Pollock and Maitland tell us much. For example, unlike our American courts today, Anglo-Saxon courts were mostly held outdoors. Our courts allow amended pleadings by litigants. In Anglo-Saxon law, as in early Rome, any mistakes in pleading were fatal to the litigant.

Once litigants get beyond the pleading stage in our courts, trial by jury is the principal means of determining truth. Anglo-Saxon courts relied on compurgation or "oath helping," whereby the defendant first swore on the Bible that he was innocent of the charge. Then he brought in "oath helpers" to "swear that his oath was 'clean.'"

While compurgation amounted to "organized lying," and favored the defendant, trial by ordeal certainly did not. As Cantor summarizes, the "motto here was not 'We'll lie through our teeth' but 'Leave it up to God to show if the defendant is guilty.'" The ordeal of cold water was apparently the most common: "The defendant was bound hand and foot and thrown into the water. If he sank he was innocent....If he floated he was declared guilty because water...would not receive a guilty person."[21]

America today has a well-developed body of civil law—especially in property, contract, and tort. Civil law in the Anglo-Saxon world was almost nonexistent. The law of property was mostly unwritten custom and local usage. Contracts were not in writing, but were confirmed instead by oath and the acceptance of money to seal the bargain. Of a modern law of contract there is no trace.

Completely unlike our law, Anglo-Saxon criminal law at first regarded "the idea of wrong to a person or his kindred" as "primary, and that of offence against the common weal secondary, even in the gravest cases." Only gradually, Pollock and Maitland say, "did the modern principles prevail, that the members of the community must be content with the remedies afforded them by law, and must not seek private vengeance." At first royal courts were reserved for "breaches of the king's peace"—acts of personal disobedience of an enemy of the king. In time, all offenses would be said to be "against the king's peace," and royal courts would become the "normal and general safeguard of the public order."[22]

Cantor tells us of three kinds of legal documents that the late Anglo-Saxons employed.[23] One was the will. The second was the charter (from *carta* in Latin, meaning "book"). Today a charter usually refers to a government act establishing a corporation. In late Anglo-Saxon England, a charter was a "big, imposing Latin document" used in the alienation of land. The third type of Anglo-

Saxon legal document was the writ. We have many important writs in American law today. The writ of *habeas corpus*, recognized in Article I of the Constitution, is the time-honored remedy to test the legality of a person's incarceration. The writ of *mandamus*, made famous in *Marbury v. Madison*, is an order by a court to an officer compelling performance of a legal duty. The writ of *certiorari* is the principal means whereby a case can be "appealed" to the Supreme Court. Originally, the writ was a brief notification that a grant of land had been made. In time, a writ came to be used more generally by the king in issuing orders.[24]

Even as early as Edward the Confessor, Maitland tells us, the division of the realm into shires (shares) "is in most respects that which at present exists." Each shire had a shire moot, a court of justice. In time the shire reeve or sheriff begins to become an increasingly important royal officer. The shire is divided into hundreds, each with its own court. Below the hundred is the township or vill. The local courts of the hundreds and shires were, as Maitland says, the principal courts of Saxon justice. Law was local; justice was local. Maitland declares that, in such a world "the men of one shire would know nothing and care nothing for the tradition of another shire."

Cantor says that the "Anglo Saxons appear to have been satisfied with their legal system." It was politically and administratively chaotic, however. It has been said that only "another Alfred or some fresh stimulus from without could have prevented this England from relapsing into the feudal confusion which was to hamper all German development for the next five centuries."[25] Edward the Confessor, the "white skinned, white haired" Edward, was not "another Alfred." In 1065, he died childless and was buried in his own creation, the newly consecrated Westminster Abbey. The *witan* "exercised their right to elect a king, choosing the wealthiest earl, Harold Godwinson," Edward's brother-in-law, as the monarch.[26]

Protesting that *he* had been named heir by Edward himself, William, Duke of Normandy, Edward's nephew, invaded England with an army of ten thousand men while Harold was preoccupied in the North repelling a Norwegian assault. In the ensuing Battle of Hastings, Harold was mortally wounded and the English were soundly defeated. "In the English ranks," wrote William's chaplain, "the only movement was the dropping of the dead."[27] The kingdom of Alfred the Great had survived attacks by Danes and Norsemen. Now, a foreign dynasty had replaced it for good.[28] And "so, not without glory, the story of Saxon England came to an end."[29]

English Law from the Conquest to Magna Carta, 1066–1215

aitland calls the Norman Conquest "an event of the utmost importance in the history of English law." Still, he goes on, "we must not suppose that English law was swept away or superseded by Norman law. We must not suppose that the Normans had any compact body of laws to bring with them. They can have had very little if any written law of their own; in this respect, they were far behind the English."[1] Victorian essayist Thomas Carlyle was wrong when he wrote that the Normans civilized "a gluttonous race of Jutes and Angles, capable of no great combinations, lumbering about in pot-bellied equanimity."[2]

The ancestors of the Normans—fierce heathen Vikings called Normani (Northmen)—had migrated into northwest France from Scandinavia in the tenth century. There, they adopted the religion and language of the French. They had few written laws and no treatises on law. As Pollock and Maitland remind us, the "England of the same period supplies us with the laws of Edward the Elder, Aethelstan, Edmund, Edgar, Aethelred, and Cnut."[3] Consequently, Maitland adds, "what settled law there was in Normandy was rather Frankish than Norse." For written law, the Normans on the eve of the Conquest turned to French documents "of great antiquity, the Lex Salica and the capitularies of the Frankish kings." Some of the traditions of that Frankish law continue in American law today. For example, Maitland tells us that the "practice of summoning a body of neighbours to swear to royal and other rights, which is the germ of trial by jury, appears in England as soon as the Normans have conquered the country, and it can be clearly traced to the courts of the Frankish kings."[4]

In short, the invading Normans "had no written law to bring with them to England, and we may safely acquit them of much that could be called jurisprudence."[5] They were, for the most part, warlike, uncultured, and illiterate, and found in England laws more developed than what they had known in Normandy. Thus, one of the first promises William made was that the English would retain their old laws. Maitland says this meant "the good old law, the law which prevailed here before England fell under the domination of the Conqueror."[6]

It would be a mistake, however, to conclude from all this preserving of Anglo-Saxon law that William was a mild-mannered republican king. He is called William the Conqueror for a reason: he conquered. After getting himself crowned king on Christmas Day in 1066—the year of what Pollock and Maitland call "the catastrophe which determines the whole future history of English law"[7]—William proceeded with the "harrying of the north," a policy of deliberate devastation. All in all, the Conquest was a "long and bloody business"—one of only two periods of widespread devastation in English history, the other being the Reformation five hundred years later.

Those who had fought for Harold forfeited their lands. In their place, William created his own aristocracy of "tenants-in-chief" who swore to perform services in return for the land he gave them, thereby laying the groundwork for the future of Anglo-American property law. These tenants-in-chief, like American "robber barons," subinfeudated the land or, in effect, rented it out to other tenants, who, in turn, pledged their services to the tenant-in-chief. This subinfeudating continued down the feudal pyramid. England was "partitioned among a foreign aristocracy."[8]

In France, the same subinfeudation "implied political weakness for the king" because, Cantor explains, "subvassals owed loyalty to the duke or count, not to the French king. William and his successors...insisted that they were the 'liege lord...of every subvassal, down to the lowliest...in the realm.' "⁹

In America, it took a civil war to achieve that centralization. In Anglo-Norman history, it took the Conquest and many centuries of strong monarchs to do much the same thing. This unity eventually permitted development of a common law.

It is important to bear in mind that all of this was just beginning under William. To ensure more centralization of law, he and his successors began to send their own royal justices around the country to hear cases in the king's name and preside over shire courts. To verify what these traveling judges were saying about who had the right to possession of land, William commissioned a gigantic inventory of all the estates of the realm—a record called *Domesday Book* because, like the last judgment of God and decisions of the American Supreme Court, there was no appeal from its unalterable decrees.

Domesday Book is one of William's most important contributions to law. It recorded the conditions of the two nations living in one country—the Norman conquerors and the Anglo-Saxon natives. One example of the uneasy coexistence of these peoples is the so-called Law of Englishry, which provided that if a dead body was found, it was presumed to be that of a Norman, unless a village could prove the dead man was English. If he was English, there was no penalty, but if Norman, heavy fines were imposed. To prove he was English, witnesses from the neighborhood would be called in to swear it. This was an early use of the jury—as a device for catching criminals, not adjudicating guilt.

Some of the legal changes William made tended in the short term to divide the English from the Normans. Trial by battle, which naturally favored the more militarily powerful Normans, was introduced. Arguably, none of this made the law "common." Over time, however, the English and the Normans intermarried and began to forge a union. Within about a century of the Conquest, the Norman flair for strong government would change things. For the first time, a well-organized national government and a central judicial system would begin to emerge in England.

In William the Conqueror's time, however, the Normans were still foreigners. They were French, and French soon became the language of the court, of law, of government, and of administration. For three centuries, English was exiled from the courts and the state, and remained almost entirely a spoken, not written, tongue.

William died shortly after the *Domesday* survey, leaving Normandy to his eldest son and England to his younger son, the redheaded William Rufus—an "ungainly squat figure without dignity or charm" who later got himself "accidentally murdered" in a forest under suspicious circumstances.[10] He was succeeded by another brother of William, who became Henry I, a well-educated but cruel monarch who introduced the punishment of drawing and quartering of traitors and the penalty of gouging out the eyes for defamation.

The picture we have of law in the time of Henry I—*Leges Henrici Primi* (*The Laws of Henry I*, 1118)—shows the local courts were very different from our courts today. Trial was still usually by ordeal, battle, or oath, not by jury; there was little uniformity; almost everything was oral, not written. Litigation was expensive and as uncertain as a game of dice.

It is also during the reign of Henry I that we get the first stage in the preservation of the common law from Romanization, a story that is of vital importance to our American constitutional heritage. The Roman law of Justinian—a law of absolutism totally alien to our American tradition of constitutional liberty—was gaining influence on the European continent. Determined to Romanize English law, clerics brought Vacarius, "one of the leading teachers of Roman law in Bologna," home of the world's first law school, to England in the 1140s "to coach them on the niceties of the Justinian system then beginning to radiate northward into France and Germany."[11]

However, this "Bolognian visitation came at a particularly unpropitious time for implementation of the Roman system in England." After Henry I's death, England experienced a civil war for "nineteen long winters when God and His angels slept"—an age when *feudalism* became another name for feuding. Finally things settled down with

Henry II—the second "Lion of Justice" and true royal founder of the common law of England, whose nobles killed the archbishop of Canterbury Thomas Becket, an event immortalized in T. S. Eliot's famous play *Murder in the Cathedral.*

Henry II and the Origins of the Common Law

To appreciate the significance of Henry II's contribution, one must begin by recalling what had and had not changed in English law under his Norman predecessors. As Cantor puts it, "most of the judicial system of the Anglo-Saxon era was perpetuated in the Norman French monarchy after 1066." What was new was a "different attitude on the part of the king and his officials toward the law." Cantor elaborates: "The Anglo-Saxon kings had mostly stood aside from the law.... Beginning with William the Conqueror, the Norman French kings and their Angevin (or Plantagenet) descendants viewed themselves as heads of the legal system, as intimately responsible for the functioning and improvement of law."[12]

In the twentieth and twenty-first centuries, American presidents see the appointment of a new Supreme Court justice as an instrument of policy. Theodore Roosevelt first made that clear when, in appointing Oliver Wendell Holmes to the High Court in 1902, he said his first concern was "the real politics of the man." American presidents today still see appointment of justices as a way to affect policy. This is similar to the new way the Norman French kings of England began to look on law after 1066—as "an instrument of royal power, as a weapon to assert their control over society."[13]

Of all the English kings who effected this changed attitude toward law, none is more important than Henry II. With him, we begin to get the important outlines of the English common law—that "accumulated mass of rights and immemorial customs" that forms the basis of our legal system. It is still far too early, with Henry II, to speak of the fully developed common law of England. This is only the origin of the common law. As yet there is no strict adherence to precedent, no stare decisis. Still, it was Henry II who, in Maitland's words, "centralized English justice"[14] and so laid the foundation for the common law development of England and America. He is surely one of the greatest kings of the Middle Ages and "one of the greatest men in English medieval history."

Henry's challenge, like America's at the end of the Revolution and again in 1865, was to unify and bring peace to a land beset by civil war. Goldwin Smith summarizes how he fulfilled this goal: "He restored order and reorganized the central government;...he extended the power of the central royal courts; he increased the use of writs and itinerant justices; he introduced the jury system as a normal part of royal court procedure; he added much to the coral reef of the common law."[15]

It would not be fair to say that Henry II was a great "legislator." Like his predecessors, his genius was for administration of law. In a land recovering from two decades of anarchy, the first step was a reorganization of the central government.

The "court" of the Norman kings, starting with the Conqueror, had consisted of his tenants-in-chief, and the king held court three times a year at great festivals where the tenants-in-chief became the Great Council of the realm, approving legislation desired by the king and advising him about policy. This Great Council is, of course, the direct ancestor of the English Parliament and the American Congress, but words like *Parliament* and *Congress* were a long way off in Norman England. Also unlike our legislatures, it was not always clear who had a right to attend these sessions, and participation was more a burden than a privilege. Just as presidents such as Lincoln have appointed political rivals to cabinet positions in order to keep them in check, Maitland says the Norman king gathered the most powerful tenants-in-chief in his council. He "keeps his eye upon them,...and measures are taken with the counsel and consent of his peers."

Over time, the king came to summon "only such of his tenants in chief as he pleased." Just as modern American presidents, especially since World War II, have relied increasingly on their White House staff and on a close circle of advisers rather than taking major policy issues to the whole cabinet much less to Congress, a smaller body of councilors begins to collect around the English kings. Top officers in this body begin to take on titles: the chief justiciar is a sort of viceroy, taking the place of the king when he is out of the country; the chancellor is at this early stage the head of a body of clerks who do the secretarial work for the king.

Under Henry I, this small body of councilors begins to become more organized and take on a life of its own. When it sits for financial purposes, it becomes the Exchequer, the first administrative department to settle down in one place and today's equivalent of our Treasury. In those days, the Exchequer—so named because its officers did their accounting at a table covered by a checkered cloth—literally had custody of the king's treasures and revenue, and it was extremely cumbersome to move all that around every time the king moved. So the custom developed of letting the Exchequer stay in London, or more precisely in Westminster, the area west of London around the abbey that Edward the Confessor had built. The Exchequer was also the first department to keep a written record of what it was doing—the Pipe Rolls, started around 1130. Eventually it came to be understood that if the Exchequer was to sit permanently in Westminster, there should be courts sitting permanently there, too. This establishment of a stationary royal court, which would function on its own, even when the king was not there, was the true beginning of the judicial system of England.

This did not have to occur in America. We did not begin our country's history with a court following the president from place to place. The Supreme Court has always been independent of the president and, except when the justices "rode the Circuit" in the early years, has always met in a fixed location. But that is because we took the English lessons already learned.

In the time of Henry II, a central royal court, called the Bench, begins to sit regularly in Westminster. In time it came to be understood that there were two sorts of law cases—those in which the king had a direct interest that were heard by a group of judges who followed the king around and came to be called King's Bench, and cases in which the king had no direct interest that were heard by judges who stayed in one fixed place and who became the Court of Common Pleas.

Henry II also intensified the practice, which began with the Conqueror and *Domesday*, of sending judges from the royal household into the countryside. Henry I had used this practice occasionally. His grandson Henry II made the practice regular and routine. Twice a year, three justices in eyre would ride into a town, transform a local court into a royal court, and investigate all manner of local problems.

In the first century of our judicial system, the circuit courts were staffed by the Supreme Court justices and the district judges who rode around each circuit, bringing law and uniformity and republican government to all regions. The framers who put that practice into the Judiciary Act of 1789 knew, of course, about the English itinerant judges of medieval times, and saw this practice as a way of nationalizing our country and unifying it, much as Henry II had done.

This English medieval practice is far more significant than modern circuit riding would suggest, however. What Henry II did by regularizing this process was to begin to build up the common law—the very heart of our Anglo-American system of law. Professor Smith summarizes the long-term consequences: "As the itinerant justices moved about England, they began to make a national common law for the whole kingdom, declaring the principles and practices of the central courts at Westminster and absorbing the best of the local law. The result, slowly achieved, was uniform law for all England, a living growth, rooted like an oak in the soil and unshattered by the storms of centuries."[16]

One of the most important issues that Henry II's traveling judges faced was the rightful possession of land. Many tenants-in-chief had been dispossessed in the troublesome days after Henry I, when "the 'king's peace' died with him." Henry II wanted to restore their rights but also to discourage them from taking the law into their own hands.

He wanted to protect these tenants in their possession of his land, but keep them as his tenants, beholden to him, giving them justice in his courts.

It is vital to the future of Anglo-American property law that Henry set out to protect possession and not ownership of land. Roman law had permitted absolute ownership (*dominium*) in land. The Norman Conquest, however, meant that, in England, only the king owned land. Everyone else, from the highest tenant-in-chief or baron to the lowest serf, only possessed it.

This seems a far cry from our modern land law. For centuries, the fee simple absolute has been the principal form of land ownership in America, and it suggests the kind of absolute ownership that the medieval English world did not know. Still, even today, lawyers do not say that a person "owns" land but rather that he or she "holds an estate in land." And there is a very real sense in which all land is, even in current America, owned by the king. If a fee simple estate "runs out of heirs," the land "escheats to the state" (in effect, returns to the king). Any time the state needs a person's land to build a highway, dam, or bridge, it can take that land by eminent domain with just compensation. In a true sense, in our world today as much as in the world of Henry II, all land ultimately is owned by the king.

It was the possession of this land, not ownership, that Henry II set out to secure. In so doing, he protected the rights of those who had valid title to land, but he also protected the right to possession of those who had no title but had been in possession for a time. White reminds us that "Henry thus protected possession, rightful and wrongful alike." As Maitland puts it, he protected "the land grabber against his victim so that land should not be grabbed in future."

Our law today also protects possession, both "rightful and wrongful alike" and "the land grabber against his victim." Under the law of adverse possession, when the statute of limitations on ejectment expires—when a person in lawful possession of land loses the right to sue another for wrongful possession of that land—the unlawful dispossessor acquires full legal right to remain on the land. Put simply, an adverse possessor eventually gains a right to possession even as against the original true "owner." Like Henry II, our law thus puts "immediate peace before the ultimate triumph of truth and justice." The peace and stability of a world in which a person living on a piece of land is entitled to expect that he can stay there is valued more highly than the truth of who really is the rightful titled property owner.

To determine who was in possession of each piece of land, Henry II totally revolutionized Anglo-American law. He made trial by jury a regular part of the procedure of the royal courts, thereby inaugurating a vital part of the common law tradition.

Maitland tells us that we "cannot find the germ of trial by jury, either in the Anglo-Saxon procedure or in the ordinary procedure of the Norman courts." It can be best located in "the prerogative procedure of the court of the Frankish kings." These monarchs had inherited many of the prerogatives of the Roman emperors. According to one of those expedients, if there was any question about whether a plot of land belonged to the crown, the Frankish king would order a "public officer to inquire into this by the oaths of the neighbors." In time, the Frankish kings granted to judges this same prerogative power to summon neighbors under oath. Maitland clarifies the significance of this development for Anglo American law: "Here seems to be just what we want as the germ of trial by jury. A body of neighbors is summoned by a public officer to testify to the truth . . . about facts and rights presumably within their knowledge."

Trial by jury is, of course, one of the pillars of Anglo-American justice. For that reason, Maitland adds, "it might at first seem a very strange thing that an institution which in its origins was peculiarly Frankish became in course of time distinctively English. In France, this inquisition procedure perished; transplanted to England, it grew and flourished, and became that trial by jury which after long centuries Frenchmen introduced into modern France as a foreign, an English institution."

The Frankish empire of which Maitland speaks had, by the time of Henry II, of course, long since gone "to wreck and ruin and feudal anarchy." But, Maitland goes on, "in one corner of its domain there [had] settled a race whose distinguishing characteristic seems to have been a wonderful power of...absorbing into its own life the best and strongest institutions of whatever race it conquered." The Normans, it must be recalled, had conquered Normandy before they conquered England. It seems perfectly natural that these Normans adopted the same "power of ordering inquisitions which had been wielded by Frankish kings."[17]

Still, before Henry II, the use of the inquisition of oaths of neighbors was "something exceptional." This is what Henry II changed. He made the inquisition procedure and thus the jury "a part of the ordinary procedure open to every litigant." In the Assizes of Clarendon, Henry called for the use of juries in certain cases brought before his itinerant justices. By the Grand Assize, the holder of a plot of land could refuse trial by battle and "put himself upon the oath of a body of twelve neighbors sworn to declare which of the two parties had the greater right to the land."[18]

The modern jury is supposed to come to the trial with no previous knowledge of the case. By contrast, the "jury" or assize of Henry's day "was a self informing rather than a trial informing one,...supposed to find out as much as it could about the facts of the case before the court met."[19] Beyond this important difference, one similarity is, of course, in the number of jurors. Today, as then, there are twelve. Cantor speculates on the reason: "Jesus had twelve apostles....If you took the four points of the compass...and multiplied them by the persons of the Holy Trinity, you got twelve."[20]

Under Henry II, "all property disputes in the shire court used the jury if a litigant was willing to buy the issuance of a royal writ to impanel the jury." Since "land constituted 90 percent of the wealth of England in 1180, the use of the assize juries to settle all property disputes in the shire court was a momentous change." Maitland tells us that, in time, this jury procedure, "once made common, spreads beyond the original bounds": "We find plaintiffs and defendants in all manner of actions purchasing from the king the right to have a recognition or inquest to determine some disputed point. By slow degrees what has been a purchasable favor becomes an ordinary right.... The new procedure slowly became the rule;... disputed questions would be settled... by trial by jury—by a jury (jurata); gradually this word came into use."[21]

Royal courts with their jury trials became more popular, and thus more frequently used. Maitland summarizes the significance of these developments: "By providing new remedies in his own court, Henry centralized English justice. From his time onward, the importance of the local tribunals began to wane; the king's own court became ever more...a court of first instance for all men and all causes. The consequence of this was a rapid development of law common to the whole land; local variations are gradually suppressed; we come to have a common law."[22]

Our Founding Fathers also helped centralize justice in America by providing for jury trials in federal cases. The Constitution in Article III and the Sixth Amendment calls for jury trials in all federal criminal cases, and Amendment Seven declares that, in "Suits at common law,... the right of trial by jury shall be preserved." This latter Amendment then goes on to state that "no fact tried by a jury shall be otherwise re-examined in any Court of the United States, than according to the rules of the common law." This common law, well known to our framers and continuing to form the backbone of our law today, was, in effect, begun in Henry II's decision to extend jury trials to all royal court cases and thus centralize justice in England. It is, from the perspective of our American legal heritage, one of this monarch's greatest contributions.

As Maitland summarizes, we "have now taken account of the doctrines whereby the royal jurisdiction had extended itself, and of the new institution [the jury] which had made royal justice preferable to all other justice." We need also to dwell on something else that Henry II did to forge the national common law system. He developed the writ system, which historians call the forms of action.

American lawyers tend to think of procedure and substance as different. Law schools offer courses in civil and criminal procedure, but they are different from the substantive law courses like torts and criminal law. In medieval England, the procedural forms *were* the law. This does not just mean that lawyers then were more precise about forms than we are today. It also means that the forms came first. The forms did not evolve from the common law substantive rules. Rather, the forms were invented first and the substantive law grew up around them. There was a law of writs before there was a law of contract, or property, or tort.

Originally, the writs were letters written by the king, at the urging of some complainant, commanding the adversary to appear in court to answer the complaint, much like a summons today. Over time, the king stopped composing these letters himself and left that task to subordinates, who began keeping blank forms and filling in the blanks. If a person wanted to get the benefit of the procedure of the royal courts—which in time meant if he wanted trial by jury— he had to pay the king for the privilege of using his court. The writ, his ticket of permission, described the case and authorized the royal court to hear it.

A classification of forms of writs developed. Each writ worked like a pass admitting suitors to the kind of justice they had paid for, and there were different kinds of pass (or writ) for different purposes. In time, common lawyers came to refer to the law of the writs and how to use them as the forms of action. The forms of action were not abolished in England until the nineteenth century, and even in modern times Maitland tells us that "the forms of action we have buried but they rule us from the grave." They rule not only the English but also Americans.

The first book on the common law, and the "first of our classical textbooks of law," according to Maitland, was essentially a discussion of forms of action. This treatise is called Glanville and was written about 1187, probably by a man named Ranulf de Glanville, who was chief justiciar of England (in Pollock and Maitland's words, "prime minister, we may say, and vicerory")[23] and a man whom Henry II trusted and who had risen to become the king's right-hand man.

Glanville focuses almost exclusively on the king's courts and their law as that of the whole realm. It is, Maitland explains, "only with the king's court that the writer deals." Like a book today about federal court jurisdiction, Glanville is a book about how to get into the king's courts and what to do when there. Canter says this is essentially the way we study law in America today: "At least half the time of first-year law students in American law schools today is still spent studying actions—that is, cases. Glanville wouldn't be surprised at what he would find if he were to sit in on a class on property in a law school today. It is still his common law."[24]

It is largely because of Glanville that we can truly say that "under Henry II, England takes for a short while the lead among the states of Europe in the production of law and of a national legal literature."[25] As popular historian Roy Strong puts it in his *Story of Britain*, that "is how Henry II would have been remembered if it were not for one man, Thomas Becket."

Becket's martyrdom had profound implications for America's legal heritage considering that the controversy grew out of the peculiar privileges the clergy enjoyed under English law. We have seen that trials by battle, introduced by the Norman kings after the Conquest, were still taking place in the Plantagenet world of Henry II. Priests, however, were excused from fighting, as well as from trial by ordeal. The only "ordeal" they had to endure was to eat a piece of bread and cheese in front of the altar. A prayer to the archangel Gabriel was believed to have the power to choke a guilty priest in this act. A clergyman who swallowed the food was presumed innocent. Even more important, a clergyman accused of crime could be punished only by an ecclesiastical court and sentenced only to be unfrocked or to do penance.

Henry's efforts to cement a common law and to extend royal jurisdiction had not provoked much opposition from many who were glad to see some of the haughty nobles humbled for the sake of public peace. But Henry's attempts to "stop appeals being made directly to Rome angered the Church and led to his fateful quarrel with the Archbishop of Canterbury."[26] Becket had been Henry's friend and chancellor when the king appointed him archbishop. Henry no doubt thought that Becket would cooperate with his plans to make the Church subservient to the Crown. In this, Henry was famously disappointed. When a church canon was acquitted of murder in an ecclesiastical court, the king demanded that the man be tried in a royal court. Becket refused, insisting that "God judges no man twice in the same matter," thereby anticipating our Fifth Amendment right not to be "subject for the same offense to be twice put in jeopardy of life or limb."

In time, Henry, who "hated his former friend all the more because he had once loved him," cursed "this turbulent priest," and four knights, inspired by those hasty words, killed the archbishop in his cathedral in Canterbury. The news of the murder spread quickly. Condemned by the court of public opinion, the king of England was forced to do penance. And so, the "simple and great folk of England saw their king, warrior and statesman on his knees before the tomb of St. Thomas of Canterbury, his back scarred with weals of penance."[27]

Henry II is said to have uttered the words "shame, shame on a conquered king" on his deathbed. And yet, as Roy Strong aptly puts it, the "truth was far different. Henry II was the greatest of all the Plantagenet kings. His bequest was good government in terms of peace, law, and order on a scale unknown to any other country in Western Europe at the time. It was a splendid inheritance."[28]

TEN

From Magna Carta to the
Origins of Parliament

Henry II gave England a common law that "would survive a worthless or absentee monarch." His son Richard the Lionhearted "spent all but a few months of his reign crusading against the Moslems in the Holy Land."[1] Then came King John, "perhaps the most detestable of English kings,"[2] who, in 1215, was forced by his barons to grant the Great Charter, known to history as Magna Carta.

Maitland calls Magna Carta a "document of the utmost importance" and "the nearest approach to an irrepealable 'fundamental statute' that England has ever had."[3] It had a profound impact on American law, playing a role in what Harvard's Bernard Bailyn calls *The Ideological Origins of the American Revolution*, the title of one of his books, as well as in the decade of American constitution-making both at the state and national levels. Even today, American and English lawyers take great interest in the document. As J. C. Holt of Cambridge tells us in his book *Magna Carta*, "the memorial at Runnymede [marking where the charter was signed] is the work of the American Bar Association, and lawyers on both sides of the Atlantic are responsible for the annual gatherings of the Magna Carta Society."[4]

Originally, Magna Carta was "less the declaration of human rights it has often been supposed to be than a statement of the feudal and legal relationship between the Crown and the barons,"[5] a treaty

113

extorted from the king by the nobles, who threatened him with the loss of his lands if he did not accept its terms. Unlike our Constitution, it is, as Maitland describes, a "long document." Unlike our Declaration of Independence, it is "no declaration in mere general terms of the rights of Englishmen, still less of the rights of men." Like our Declaration, it "goes through the grievances of the time one by one and promises redress."

Magna Carta is not new law. It is a restoration of old law. As Maitland puts it, the "cry has been not that the law should be altered, but that it should be observed, in particular that it should be observed by the king." And this fact is at the heart of the legacy of Magna Carta for American constitutionalism. It confirms that the king—or president, in our case—is bound by the law.

In one famous phrase of Magna Carta, "no free man shall be taken or imprisoned or disseissed or outlawed or exiled or in any way destroyed, save by the lawful judgment of his peers or the law of the land." This clause is said to be the origin of "due process of law," one of the most litigated clauses in the American Constitution today. Another clause in the Great Charter says that Common Pleas may not follow the king but must be held in a fixed place. In America, this same clause is the ancestor of our doctrine of the independence of the judiciary. Article III of our Constitution thus draws its spirit from Magna Carta when it states that the "Judges ... shall hold their Offices during good Behaviour, and shall, at stated Times, receive for their Services, a Compensation, which shall not be diminished during their Continuance in Office."

From 1215 to 1787, when our Constitution was framed, the history of Magna Carta "is a history of repeated reinterpretation." Holt speaks of the "myth of *Magna Carta*, that interpretation of it which gives it qualities which the men of 1215 did not intend." "Lawful judgment of his peers," for example, was, in time, interpreted to mean "trial by jury"; "No free man" became "no man of whatever estate or condition he may be."[6]

Four centuries after 1215, the great seventeenth-century English jurist Sir Edward Coke reinstated Magna Carta as a legal document of great importance by expanding the word "liberties" in the Charter to mean "individual liberty." Inspired by Coke and others, Parliament argued in the Petition of Right in 1628 that "*Magna Carta* established grounds for the writ of *Habeas Corpus*," an institution later preserved and maintained by Article I of the American Constitution.

We will see later that, for the British, though not at all for us in America, Coke's ideas about fundamental law were largely discarded in the English late-seventeenth and early-eighteenth-century dedication to parliamentary sovereignty, a commitment clarified by Sir William Blackstone, who was famous both for his commentary on Magna Carta and his *Commentaries on the Laws of England*, one of the most influential books in the American colonies. Still, as Holt puts it, this "marked not the end but yet another stage in the history of *Magna Carta*." From this point, "in England it became the political property of the radicals." And from the radicals in England, it

> also survived in America... [where] the fight was not in defense of law and Parliament against the king, but for the rights of the colonists against both king and Parliament.... And just as the Charter was claimed by the English radicals as a natural birthright, so in America some of its principles came to be established as individual rights, enforceable against authority in all its forms, whether legislative, executive, or judicial, whether represented by Crown, governor, or council, or later by state and federal government.[7]

The Charter was "embodied in the legal structure of the early colonies." As state after state wrote its own new constitution, the phrases "law of the land" and "due process of law" were included. Magna Carta survived, "alongside natural law by being raised to the same universal terms." As Holt concludes, if "the matter is left in broad terms of sovereign authority on the one hand and the subject's rights on the other, this was the legal issue at stake in the fight against John [in 1215], against Charles I [in the English Civil War of the 1640s] and in the resistance of the American colonists to George III."[8]

Magna Carta is certainly the most important constitutional development of the reign of King John (reigned 1199–1216). It is during the reign of his successor, Henry III, that we begin to hear the first attacks on what in today's legal world is called judicial activism. "It is more and more seen...that the judges while professing to declare the law are in reality making law," Maitland says. Today, Supreme Court justices such as Antonin Scalia and legal scholars like Mark Levin attack judges who "make rather than interpret law." As Levin puts it in *Men in Black: How the Supreme Court Is Destroying America*, critics maintain that activist judges "have abused their constitutional mandate by imposing their personal prejudices and beliefs on the rest of society."

Many judges certainly do "make" law in America today, and so did many in the time of Henry III. One of those men was Henry of Bratton, known to history as Bracton, who wrote a famous treatise on the laws of England sometime between 1250 and 1260. Bracton, as the treatise is known, is a survey of the common law, and, like Glanville, of the writ system. Bracton gives us a "moving picture of the law in action," and reading him we see that the law of his day was, like our own, complicated, expensive, and full of jargon.

Pollock and Maitland famously call Bracton "the flower and crown of English jurisprudence" and add that it is "Romanesque in form, English in substance." Bracton had studied the writings of the great Italian lawyer Azo of Bologna and Justinian's *Corpus Juris*, getting his idea of what a law book should look like from these Roman law sources. But, Maitland goes on, "the substance of Bracton's work is English." "The main matter of the treatise is genuine English law laboriously collected out of the plea rolls of the English court,...and of any desire to Romanize the law we must absolutely acquit him."[9]

But if Bracton was so well versed in Roman law, why didn't he try to "Romanize the law" of England? More to the point, why did an

English common law, separate from the Roman law tradition, survive? This is one of the greatest questions of legal history.

While the common law was developing in England, Europe was falling under the influence of Roman law. Earlier we mentioned the revival of Roman law in the universities on the continent in the twelfth and thirteenth centuries. This revival also spread to England through its two great new universities, Oxford and Cambridge. English law "pleaders" or lawyers who appear and argue in court—what Americans call litigators and what the British today call barristers—did not primarily learn law in the universities, however. They learned it in the Inns of Court.

We do not know exactly when the Inns of Court started in England. We know they existed by the time of Chaucer (1340–1400) and that they probably emerged shortly after Bracton. Law schools needed a place for their students to live in London, so they took over four failing inns and remade them into training clubs. Soon, there were (and there still are) four such Inns of Court in London: Gray's Inn, Lincoln's Inn, the Middle Temple, and the Inner Temple.

Cantor tells us that the "Inns of Court combined functions that are divided among three different agencies in the United States—they are law schools, they are fraternities for barristers and provide club houses for them, and they admit graduates to the bar." Most important, it was work done in chambers, as an apprentice to a prominent law pleader, that determined the future career of the pupil. In other words, it quickly became the tradition in England that some lawyers received their training in what we today would call law offices—where only English common law and the practical reality of writs and pleadings were the order of the day—rather than at universities where Roman law ideas were being bandied about by scholars and clerics.

These Inns of Court saved England from Roman law. As we have seen, the Roman law that was being taught in the universities and spreading through Europe was the law of the Roman Empire—a regime of absolutism in which the king was above the law. It is of vital importance that the English common law resisted this idea. At

Harvard Law School, the words of Bracton are carved in stone: the king is "not under Man, but under God and the Law." And the English common law clung to this idea because it escaped Romanization.

But if the king was "under the law," was there any way of enforcing that law against him? As Pollock and Maitland say, "there is no established orderly method whereby this can be accomplished, and the right to restrain an erring king, a king who should be God's vicar, but behaves as the devil's vicar, is rather a right of revolution."[10] Writing in his *Constitutional History*, Maitland is more emphatic:

> And now what was the king's legal position? ...Against him the law had no coercive process; there was no legal procedure whereby the king could either be punished or compelled to make redress....On the other hand, it is by no means admitted that the king is above the law....The king is below no man, but he is below God and the law; law makes the king; the king is bound to obey the law, though if he breaks it, his punishment must be left to God.[11]

Maitland goes on to say that, to the modern student of law, this seems an absurd contradiction. Either "the king is sovereign or no; if he be sovereign, then he is not legally below the law; ...on the other hand, if he is below the law, then he is not sovereign." Someone or something else is sovereign. This is the right way of looking at it, Maitland explains, if, as positivists, we regard all law as command and say that "in every state there must be some man or some body of men above all law." The positivism of Thomas Hobbes had not yet appeared, however. And, Maitland adds, "well for us is it that this was so, for had they looked about for some such sovereign man or sovereign body, ...there can be little doubt that our king would have become an absolute monarch, a true sovereign ruler."[12]

Who, then, was to make the law? By the fourteenth century, the English were beginning to answer that "for new laws the consent of the estates of the realm" is needed. This increasingly meant not the king alone but the king and his greater council, which was slowly coming to be understood as Parliament.

As Goldwin Smith puts it, the "growth of the English Parliament is one of the capital facts of modern civilization."[13] Still, it is easy for us to imagine that Parliament had a steady rise, inspired by love of freedom. Instead, Cambridge's R. J. White reminds us, the "story is confusing in its detail and may seem disappointing in its outcome." Historians, for example, sometimes see in the thirteenth and four-teenth centuries "the take-off for an effective institutional check on royal despotism and misrule, the first treads in a flight of stairs lead-ing upwards and onwards to the latter-day landings of constitutional government." The reality, however, White goes on, is that "Parliamen-tary government, indeed Parliament itself, sprang not so much from baronial opposition [to the king] as from the royal prerogative and the king's necessities."

The first necessity, of course, was a council. "Counsel, advice, consultation is as important to a king as money and arms," White reminds us. As we have seen, from earliest times in English history "the king's Council was a body of men whom the king summoned because he thought their advice would be useful, or whose opinions and interests it would be unwise, even dangerous, to neglect. It had no competence which did not arise from his own free will, or preroga-tive. It could do nothing that he did not wish it to do, and it had no existence apart from him."[14]

Under the Normans it is not yet clear that the consent of the Great Council is "necessary for taxation" or that "the majority of an assem-bly could bind a recalcitrant minority." Fundamental principles of a representative assembly like our Congress were not yet in operation.[15]

A very important step toward the sort of representative govern-ment we know today occurred, however, in the reign of Henry II. The king "obtained from a great national council a promise of a tithe for the crusade" and he employed a representative "jury of neighbors" to determine how much each person's contribution to that tithe, or tax, would be. Thus, as Maitland concludes, "taxation and representation are brought into connection—the individual is assessed by his neighbors, by a jury representing his parish, and so in some sort representing him. The idea that representation should accompany taxation gains ground." In our Constitution today, "all Bills for raising Revenue... originate in the House of Representatives," which means that all tax laws have to be introduced first in the house of Congress that is closest to the people—the one that is the most direct heir of the representative assembly that was beginning to emerge in England in the thirteenth century.

In that century, the "first English king to reinforce his Council with non-feudal elements—knights and burgesses—was Edward I (reined 1272–1307)."[16] Like Shakespeare's Lear, Edward I was "every inch a king," the "most eminent 'actor of majesty' before the appearance of Henry VIII in 1509,"[17] the warrior who conquered the Welsh, battled the Scots, and hanged William Wallace (*Braveheart*). From the perspective of American constitutionalism, Edward I is the "English Justinian." Maitland explains this "not very happy" metaphor: "It is something like a comparison between childhood and second childhood. Justinian... [gave] immutable form to a system which had already seen its best days.... [Edward] legislated for a nation which was only just beginning to have a legal system of its own."[18]

It was, Maitland adds, "the necessity for raising money" that forced Edward "to negotiate with all classes of his realm" and led him to call ever broader and more "representative" assemblies. Public policy was increasingly complex and expensive. Edward, seeking approval for policies and money to support them, called more and more representatives of what Smith calls the "rural and town middle class" to attend his Great Council.[19] By this point, the word *Parliamentum* (from the French *parler*, "to talk") was coming into use, replacing earlier terms like *Concilium* and *Colloquium*.

In the year 1295, the need for money to wage war led Edward to summon what history now calls the Model Parliament, which became the standard for all future Parliaments and for the American Congress and representative assemblies around the world. Maitland makes the necessary elaboration: "A body constituted in this manner is a parliament; what the king enacts with the consent of such a body is a statute....Thus, before the end of the thirteenth century the national assembly is...becoming an assembly of the estates of the realm,...[of] clergy, barons, and commons, those who pray, those who fight, those who work."[20]

White is correct to say that the English Parliament "was as much the achievement of Edward I as the triumph of the common law was the achievement of Henry II." Still, as White explains, all this was not "the culmination of a deliberate process of experiment and planning." Edward and the other English monarchs who enlarged Parliament were not publicly minded statesmen engaging in a "'controlled experiment,' building up stage by stage a comprehensive representative assembly." Like the common law, Parliament was "the offspring of the royal prerogative." Like the juries of Henry II's courts, the representatives of Parliament were summoned by royal writ because it was in the king's interest to summon them, not because doing so fulfilled a principle of popular rule. As White puts it, "the "English people acquired the habit of self government not because they had a talent for self government but because they had a Parliament."[21]

This Parliament became the source of the first English statutes, "superior to customs or to common law,...the law of all the land."[22] Our Constitution similarly provides that acts of Congress passed in pursuance of the Constitution "shall be the supreme Law of the Land."

Maitland reminds us that the reign of Edward I "is a unique period in the history of our law" primarily because of its extraordinary legislative activity. Like the first Hundred Days of FDR's presidency, the first thirteen years of Edward I's reign saw much legislation—so much that "more was done to settle and establish the distributive justice of the kingdom [in those thirteen years] than in all the ages since that time put together."[23]

The most important statutes of Edward I's reign are in the area of property law. By the statute De Donis Conditionalibus, it became easier for barons to keep land in the same bloodline. A practice of entailing land was accepted, and this "was a major reason for the maintenance of large estates in England through several centuries." The fee tail, as it came to be called, continued in America, despite the fierce opposition of antiaristocratic lawyers such as Thomas Jefferson, and it is a practice still in use, though in a much modified form, in some American jurisdictions.

Statutes like De Donis are the "basis of our land law." More significantly, they begin to check the growth of the common law, as Maitland explains: "Henceforward the common law grows much more slowly, . . . hampered at every turn by statute . . . [and the] principle that changes in the law are not to be made without the consent of parliament."

This change had important consequences for American law. Although we are a common law country, our law, like that in England under Edward I, is heavily statutory. Since the turn of the twentieth century, there has been what one legal scholar has called an "orgy of statute making." The average state in the United States today has as many statutes as the average civil law nation on the continent of Europe.[24]

This dominance of statutes has its roots in the Parliaments of Edward I. But there is another perhaps even more important legacy of the explosion of statutes during his reign. Maitland tells us that, not long after Edward I, "English lawyers are no longer studying Roman law." The statutory outpouring of Edward I's reign completed the immunization from Roman law begun by the Inns of Court. Once again it is Maitland who elaborates this most clearly for us: "To any further Romanization of English law, a stop was put by Edward's legislation. The whole field of law was now so much covered by statute that the study of Roman law had become useless. . . . The consequence is that from the beginning of Edward's reign, English law becomes always more insular, and English lawyers become more and more utterly ignorant of any law but their own."

Such ignorance may remind us of the attitude of many contemporary American lawyers, but one wonders how it can be a reason for national pride. Still, it bears repeating there is considerable and long-lasting advantage—for both America and England—in the common law's rejection of Roman law: "Thus English law was saved from Romanism; by this we lost much—but we gained much also. The loss, we may say, was juristic; if our lawyers had known more of Roman law, our law—in particular our land law—would never have become the unprincipled labyrinth that it became;—the gain, we may say, was constitutional, was political;—Roman law here as elsewhere would sooner or later have brought absolutism in its train."

Any student who has had even the shortest introduction to the law of real property in America will understand what Maitland means by the "unprincipled labyrinth" of our land law, a complex tangle of apparently outdated concepts and abstruse terminology. But again we have to keep in mind the gain. If English law had become Romanized, Bracton's principle that the king is under the law would have had no place. The growing consensus was that kings could not tax except by the "common consent of the realm" or, in other words, could not tax without Parliament's approval. This would not have been possible under a Romanized English law.

It was increasingly understood that the king could not, on his own, make new law for the whole realm. Beyond that, however, the world of law under Edward I looks decidedly unlike our own. It was not by any means clear that the commons such as it was had any right to share in the making of legislation. Although the Parliament was acquiring the right to approve taxes, the king was not "nearly so dependent on taxation as a modern government is." He had other sources of income, including profits from his royal courts, which had gained a practical monopoly on the administration of justice.[25]

These royal courts met in Westminster Hall—a large building

that is part of the Palace of Westminster, next to where Parliament now meets. This building dates back to 1099 and was the home of the English courts for centuries until they moved to the Royal Courts of Justice in the Strand in 1882. What is striking about Westminster Hall even today is that it is all one big hall. There were not separate rooms for the separate courts. Each court occupied part of the room and was marked off by a wooden bar at which the attorneys stood (hence the term *bar*). In the center of each court, there was a large table covered with a green cloth at which the judges sat. Each court was scarcely out of earshot of the others, and speakers had to shout to be heard not only over the voices of the judges and litigants in the other courts but also over the noise of mobs of lawyers, shopkeepers, pickpockets, and sightseers who thronged through the hall at all times. All this seemed to suit the English very well, as they kept it that way for about five hundred years. In time, the positions of the courts became so fixed—Common Pleas in one place, King's Bench in another—that it would be unthinkable to move a court. One judge refused to move a few inches to avoid the draft from the door because doing so would violate Magna Carta.

In recollecting that these courts remained from the time of Edward I to the nineteenth century, we must take note of the great significance of Edward's legal accomplishments. By 1307, when he died, nearly all the institutions that were to govern England for the next five hundred years, and the ancestors of all the institutions that continue to govern England and America today, were already in place:

> In the first place, there is the kingship; this is the centre of the centre. Then there is that assembly of the three estates of the realm, clergy, lords, and commons to which the name parliamentum is coming to be specifically appropriated. Then again the king has a council (concilium) which is distinct from Parliament, and he has high offices of state, a chancellor, treasurer.... Then again he has courts, courts which in a peculiar way are his courts, ... Kings Bench, the Common Bench, the Exchequer.

Like Pisistratus, the great constitution maker of ancient Athens, Edward knew that to do what he wanted, he "needed the support of the humbler classes of the nation." Widening his Great Council, he thus set in motion a train of events that neither he nor any of his contemporaries could possibly have foreseen. In time, "butchers, bakers, tailors, and drapers" came to sit with "earls, knights, bishops, and abbots" in Parliament. Few of these men wanted to be there. They were there because the king wanted them there. As Halliday puts it, "he merely wanted their money, though it was also desirable that they should agree to part with it, for 'what touches all...should be approved by all.' It was a maxim that was to have important consequences."[26]

Later, in the next century, Parliament came to be even more important. Embroiled in a Hundred Years War with France, kings including Edward III turned to Parliament for money. Parliament began attaching conditions to its grants, much as the American Congress does today. It soon came to be understood that Parliament could refuse money grants and thus compel the monarch, through his financial dependence, to follow their policy. In the last decades of the fourteenth century, Parliament developed the modern technique of impeachment—to hold the king's ministers directly responsible to Parliament for their actions. The House of Commons would present the minister before the House of Lords for a trial. The penalty could be death. In this way, a king could do no wrong, but his ministers could.

With these developments, then, we are truly on the verge of the modern legal world. But there was one last great test for the common law. It had survived the Middle Ages. It had survived the Crusades, the Black Plague, the Hundred Years War with France, and the incompetence of many kings. But then came another line of English kings who brought England closer to despotism and closer to Roman law than ever before. That line of kings is called the Tudors, and the greatest of the Tudor kings was Henry VIII.

In the next chapters, we will continue the saga of the developing

English constitution and the roots of American law with a look at the Tudors and how the successors of the Tudors, the Stuarts, came to fight Parliament and plunge the country into civil wars and revolutions that changed Anglo-American constitutionalism forever. We will also discuss three great figures of the seventeenth and eighteenth centuries and their influence on America—John Locke, who gave us the idea of prerogative and the labor theory of property; William Blackstone, who gave us the idea of legislative supremacy; and Sir Edward Coke, the English jurist who took the common law seriously and tried to save the idea that the king is under the law.

ELEVEN

Henry VII and the Foundations of Tudor Constitutionalism

The age of the Tudors in England is the making of the modern English nation. Cambridge historian G. R. Elton puts it succinctly in *England under the Tudors*. In the 118 years from the accession of the first Tudor, Henry VII, to the death of the last Tudor, Elizabeth I, "England changed...[becoming] wealthier, more firmly unified, more fully national, more modern in her outlook, and properly equipped to play her part in the wider world which had also emerged."[1] After the Tudors, England was ready to take her place among the great nations of history.

Historians tell us that the Tudor age began with Henry Tudor, when, in 1485, at Bosworth Field, he defeated and killed Richard III, the infamous hunchbacked king of Shakespearean fame who had allegedly murdered the princes in the Tower. Henry Tudor became Henry VII of England, ending decades of the Wars of the Roses, the "thirty-year contest between the White Rose of York and the Red Rose of Lancaster...for possession of the English crown."[2]

These wars had disrupted the whole legal structure of the realm. As Elton puts it, they resulted in "the growth of an unstable social structure thriving on disorder and lawlessness, and in the rapidly increasing weakness of the Crown."[3] Before the 1300s under Henry II, as we have seen, the English common law had been off to a good start. Despite his ill-fated quarrel with Becket, Henry II had given England a newly centralized court system. Throughout the high Middle Ages,

"England was almost the model of a monarchy,...remarkably free from the destructive centrifugal forces which feudalism released" elsewhere. But in the fourteenth century, while Chaucer was writing his *Canterbury Tales*, the English monarchy went into decline. Weak kings fought a long and costly war with France. The bubonic plague wiped out a huge portion of the English population. By the 1400s, two rival families—of Lancaster and of York—were fighting for the throne. England was in civil war.

This civil war was a great challenge to the common law, just as the civil wars that had followed the reign of Henry I had been. Government seemed to be evaporating. Blood feuds were returning. "Intimidation and chicanery supplanted...the king's peace." "Rebellion had become a habit, treason an occupation."[4] As historian S. T. Bindoff puts it, by

> 1485 Englishmen had grown wearily accustomed to a polity in which rival factions contended for the Crown and "he who lost the day lost the kingdom also."...A Crown which had become a football was ceasing to be a referee, and a game which begins by doing without a referee runs a risk of finishing without a ball. Right was beginning to yield to might at all levels and in all relationships of society, and four centuries of heroic effort by kings and statesmen to establish the reign of law seemed in danger of being brought to nought amid a surfeit of kings and a shortage of statesmen.[5]

This was the chaotic England that Henry VII's victory over Richard III at Bosworth Field put to an end in 1485. Yet no one then knew that England and English law stood on the threshold of a new era of success. Bindoff puts it well: "Was the victor of Bosworth to be just another king,...captain of a sinking ship?...Or was he, after all, the Messianic statesman who could deliver both Crown and Kingdom from bondage to a bankrupt political system?"

Henry VII thus faced a task as difficult as any of his predecessors. He had to find a way to restore the rule of law. To do this, Henry understood at once, that "the civil wars would have to be ended once and for all." As Elton comments, to "the preservation of law and order, the security of the realm,...he applied all his high intelligence and tenacity of will.[6] At the same time, Henry had to hold the support of classes of people most directly interested in maintaining this law and order. He had to win the support of the lesser gentry of the estates and the merchants of the towns—to "call them a middle class is to define them much more precisely than is proper"—who had little interest in noble factions and were ready to welcome any king, as long as he was strong. It was, as Elton says, this "landed gentry...who formed the bulk of the politically conscious and active population, and whose support had to be kept secure."[7]

In some ways, Henry's role, then, was not unlike that of our own Founders. The Constitution would not have survived had they not established order and won the support of a large bulk of the population. Constitutional historian Edward S. Corwin talks about this in *The Higher Law: Background of American Constitutional Law,* saying the Constitution won because of the prosperity it brought. Similarly, the Tudors won because the Wars of the Roses were followed by relative peace and prosperity under Henry VII.

To achieve this peace, Henry did not replace a legal system with a new one. He restored the vigor of the old. As Goldwin Smith puts it, Henry's genius was that he "constantly sought to strengthen and invigorate existing institutions, central and local, to make them instruments of royal power."[8] Elton says the task of the "new dynasty essentially consisted in getting back to heights already reached 200 years earlier....A king strong and independent enough to re-assert the inherent powers of the English crown would find the means all ready to hand, only waiting to be used."[9]

When Elton says an English king could "find the means all ready to hand," his words cry out for comparison to the American presidency. Like Henry, a president coming into office after a period of weakness can also find all the means "ready to hand, only waiting to be used." Franklin Roosevelt came to the White House in the middle of the Great Depression, when public confidence in the government, the presidency, and the capitalist system was at an all-time low. Similarly, Ronald Reagan came to the White House after seven years of Watergate and weakness; the public had simply stopped believing that a president could both tell the truth and get the job done. Just as Henry VII revolutionized the English monarchy, so both Roosevelt and Reagan revolutionized the presidency. Just as Henry VII convinced his subjects that an English king could once again bring peace, so Roosevelt and Reagan won unprecedented reelection landslides that testified to the confidence of the American people in their leadership. Perhaps most important, like Henry VII, both Roosevelt and Reagan found the means for their revolutions "ready to hand" on their inauguration in an institution called the presidency with express and implied powers, some of which had been used effectively in the past and could be used again. In the case of Henry VII, he found the monarchy to be an institution with equally strong express and implied powers, which some of his predecessors had, as we have seen, used effectively.

Elton says in his book that "English government in the middle ages was truly the king's government." American government today is truly, as Walter Bagehot called it more than a century ago, "presidential government." But, Elton goes on, "the king and his retinue were always moving about." The increasingly complex machinery of government needed permanent residence. Over time, therefore, you get the emergence of more or less permanent departments, each going "out of court." "The exchequer or financial department led the way in the middle of the twelfth century," Elton reminds us, "to be followed by the courts of the common law."[10]

Our national government has undergone a similar though more rapid transformation. The first Congress established three executive departments—Treasury, State, and War. President Washington appointed secretaries to head each of the departments, and increasingly turned to them for counsel. The modern American "cabinet" was thus born.[11]

Like the departments of American government, the king's offices began, in the Middle Ages, to acquire a permanence of their own. In time, powerful barons sought to dominate the king by controlling these offices. To counter this, the kings began to rely more on their immediate "household" or inner circle—"the body...known to history as the 'council.'"[12]

Similarly, two systems of administration grew up in American government, too. As presidents increasingly found their agendas for change frustrated by departments bogged down in bureaucracy, they turned to an ever-expanding inner White House staff. Presidents in the last fifty years have often relied on their National Security advisers more than their Departments of State and Defense in making foreign policy.

The White House staff is composed of officers who rarely get an opportunity to advise the president and others who routinely "have the ear" of the chief executive. Similarly, the king's council came to be "further subdivided into the small number who received regular and frequent summonses [to meet and advise the king] and the majority who attended only once or twice, or at long intervals," says Elton.[13] Thus, there emerged "an inner ring of more important, more influential, more powerful counselors, commonly in attendance on the king and forming the active ministry." It was, Elton says, on the "hidden springs" of this inner council—predecessor of the Privy Council—"that government really depended." In the years before the Tudors, however, this inner council or "household" had declined in power. Witnesses of weak kings had "stressed the need for the crown to work through those public seals and departments over which the magnates could exercise a measure of control." "The decline of the household went hand in hand with the decline of the crown."[14] And yet, Elton goes on, even then "the household potential in government was not destroyed; it was only left to rust." The "motive power contained in the king's household—dormant not dead—only needed reviving."

An American president's success or failure is often determined by his choice of his closest advisers. Henry VII's success was largely due to the individuals he picked for his inner circle. In place of great nobles, "Henry drew his leading counselors from men of lower rank and smaller fortune" who owed their offices "less to their titles than to their kinship or fidelity to the king."[15] Like the Conqueror before him and every great American president, Henry VII chose counselors who were above all loyal to him.

Of course, if counselors are too loyal to the chief, they can exercise no restraint on him. Indeed, it is common to remark that Henry VII's council exercised no restraint on him. Maitland tells us that Henry did not "bring the weightiest matters before the council," which was thus left merely to "register foregone conclusions." The mistake, however, is to assume that such a change meant a weaker council. "Its power," Maitland reminds us, actually "increases, but this merely means an increase of the royal power." The council under the Tudors, like the White House staff under our strongest presidents, "is powerful against all others, but weak against the king."[16] Bindoff notes that Henry's choice of his counselors "was matched by his absolute control of their activities. The council was entirely dependent upon him. It could do nothing of its own motion. Under a Henry VI this would have meant that the council did little or nothing; under a Henry VII it meant that there was little that the council did not do.... The twin characteristics of the Council [were] complete dependence upon the king and omnicompetence under him."[17]

Elton reminds us that the functions of the council were threefold: "to advise the king in matters of policy, to administer the realm, and to adjudicate upon cases brought before it by petition."[18] Like the White House staff, the council's first two functions meant formulating policies for war and the economy and supervising local administration. It was, however, in the activities of the third function, the adjudication of cases, that the council took on powers that would lead to a darker chapter in the history of the English monarchy. Through these powers, as Elton puts it, Henry and his council "elevated prerogative to the first place in his political vocabulary."[19]

To appreciate this judicial evolution, it must be noted that, by the time of the Tudors, the common law system, "one of the glories of

England...had become rigid while circumstances changed." The procedure had become "slow, highly technical, and very expensive"—a "cumbrous machine," as Maitland puts it. Even the jury was proving a source of embarrassment; juries "could be intimidated or bribed or packed."[20]

In such an atmosphere, it is not surprising that many litigants discovered that they could not "get justice" in the common law courts. Increasingly, those who could not win "at law" began petitioning the king for special relief. The kings felt a duty to do something about these petitions because of their coronation oath to "do equal and right justice." But the petitions became so numerous—such as petitions for *certiorari* to the Supreme Court today—that the king began referring them to his chancellor, who had replaced the chief justiciar as the king's first minister, chief legal adviser, and most learned member of the council.[21]

The chancellor's review of these petitions eventually led to the Court of Chancery, which administered a system of justice known as equity, a supplement to the common law. In Chancery, proceedings were less formal. Pleading was in English, the vernacular, as opposed to legal French or Latin, the languages still used in common law courts. In Chancery, there was no jury; justice was faster and less expensive; and the doors were always open.

By the reign of Henry VII, Chancery was one of the established courts of justice, not a court of law but a court of conscience. The chancellor was not bound by precedent or rules. Each chancellor "assumed a considerable liberty of deciding causes according to his own notions of right and wrong." He was judge and jury, dispensing justice—or, as Aristotle would have said, correcting justice through equity to adapt the generality of law to individual cases. In short, by the fifteenth century, English law consisted of common law supplemented by equity, "the one administered by the old courts, the other by the new Court of Chancery."[22]

We do not have separate courts of equity in America today, and they were abolished in England in 1875. There are references to law and equity in the U.S. Constitution, however. Article III proclaims that the "judicial Power shall extend to all Cases in Law and Equity." Amendment VII declares that, in "Suits at common law,...the right of trial by jury shall be preserved."[23] American courts can and do "sit in equity," which means they hear civil cases in which the remedy sought is not the ordinary remedy of damages (money) but a judicially more creative one, like an injunction. In this way, American courts exercise much the same power that the English Court of Chancery did, providing remedies that the common law did not.

Chancery dealt only with civil cases, but the council had acquired a criminal jurisdiction distinct from and superior to that of the ordinary common law courts. By Henry VII's reign, the council could "punish those offenses which the courts of common law were incompetent to punish."[24] Like our grand jury, it could "summon witnesses to establish the truth" and "inflict penalties such as imprisonment and confiscation of property not open to the common law."[25]

Over time, the council took to holding these criminal court sessions in a room in the palace of Westminster called the Star Chamber, so named because of the stars painted on the ceiling. In time we get the Court of Star Chamber, which Bindoff calls "the council's most celebrated offspring" and "the busiest, most formidable, and most popular law court in the kingdom."

In Star Chamber, an accused would enjoy none of the procedural safeguards that we have in America today. According to our Sixth Amendment, the accused has the right to a "speedy and public trial by an impartial jury." There was no trial by jury in Star Chamber. There was no equivalent of our Fifth Amendment privilege against compulsory self-incrimination or against double jeopardy. There was no equivalent of our Sixth Amendment right of the accused to "confront the witnesses against him." The defendant in a Star Chamber proceeding "often did not see the witnesses against him" and "was not permitted to cross-examine" them. Perhaps most significantly, there was no equivalent of our Eighth Amendment prohibition on "cruel and unusual punishment." Star Chamber used torture. Indeed, the accused "might be sentenced to any kind of punishment except death."[26]

We will see that, in the century that followed the Tudors, Star Chamber came to be hated as an oppressive symbol of despotism—and it was still vividly remembered that way in the 1700s by the American colonists. In the celebrated seditious libel trial of New York printer John Peter Zenger, who was accused but then famously acquitted by a jury after printing attacks on the royal governor, Zenger's defense attorney called on the judge not to impose a procedural obstacle reminiscent of Star Chamber. In the decades after this trial, the American revolutionaries would compare Star Chamber to the summary proceedings George III was using to oppress the colonists. They wanted the rights of Englishmen restored to them in much the same way that those rights had been restored in the mother country with the abolition of Star Chamber in 1641. In many respects, the American Revolution was a war fought to give Americans the same legal rights that the English had won over the course of many centuries and won back with the abolition of Star Chamber in the 1600s.

During the reign of Henry VII, however, all this is still far in the future. In his time, Star Chamber, we may frankly say, was not abused. Rather, it was "an admirable and efficient instrument in the restoration of order and respect for the law," which helped the king to subdue the nobles.

Another strategy Henry used to weaken the nobles was financial. We must always keep in mind that Henry VII was to England what a self-made millionaire is to his corporation. Above all else, Henry knew that to have his way, he had to pay his way. To amass wealth, he pressured the great barons to cede property to him. Goldwin Smith describes how he did so: "If a noble lived well, he was informed that he could surely afford to make a gift to the king; if he lived poorly, he was told that he must be saving enough to do the same thing."[27]

Henry's use of financial pressure and Star Chamber all but destroyed the old nobility of England, much as William the Conqueror's military deeds had destroyed the Saxon nobility half a millennium earlier. In their place, Henry turned to small gentry and town merchants—men who had been trained at Oxford or Cambridge and learned law in the Inns of Court. This was a new nobility, a "new Tudor aristocracy."

There is an obvious parallel here to Pisistratus, the early Athenian "tyrant" who helped break the power of the nobles by enlisting the support of the common people, thereby setting Athens on the path to democracy and empire. There is also a parallel, in American history, to presidents such as FDR, who, like Pisistratus and Henry VII, was a patrician who championed the cause of the "have-nots" to break the power of the elite—or what Roosevelt called "the money changers in the temple."

Pitting class against class much as Roosevelt would do, Henry VII turned to this new gentry to recruit his council and even the famous royal bodyguards, or Yeomen of the Guard, the Tudor equivalent of our Secret Service. Most important, however, Henry turned to this new rising gentry class to staff his local administration and to aid in the enforcement of the law.

Law enforcement was a top priority for Henry, as it is for any mayor, governor, or president who takes office in an atmosphere of rising crime. When an American chief executive faces a crime wave, his first inclination is to press for more "tough on crime" legislation—like laws mandating the death penalty. In Henry VII's time, however, as Elton puts it, "the existing laws against violence sufficed." There were, consequently, "remarkably few [new] statutes." Instead, Henry saw that "what was needed was energetic enforcement" in "suppressing those whose improper power had threatened the peace of the country."[28]

We cannot really imagine how much that peace was threatened in a world without much local authority. The only modern parallel would have to be the gang wars of the inner cities. As Elton reminds us, until "the creation of a regular police force in the nineteenth century, England remained a country of ready violence. Every dispute turned too easily to bloodshed." Medieval England had relied on sheriffs and feudal courts to keep this violence under control. But with "the decline of the sheriff, the decay of the old popular courts of hundred and shire," a new institution began to take on importance—the justices of the peace.

When we use the term *justice of the peace*, we tend to think of someone who performs a marriage ceremony. Maitland tells us that in England the term is first applied to knights of the shire who were appointed, as far back as the thirteenth century, to "keep the peace." By the time of the Tudors, they are appointed by the king and have authority to put down riots, arrest offenders, and indict and try persons by jury.[29]

Henry VII and his successors "worked this admirable institution for all—and indeed for more than—it was worth." Like the Roman censors—and perhaps also like the editors and publishers of today's leading media outlets, in print, on the air, and on the Web—those justices of the peace (JPs) came to be "the censors of practically every other official or institution…in the fields of economics, morals, and manners."[30]

Henry VII gave these justices enlarged powers, providing backbone for the administration of the law and a "political apprenticeship" by which the new class shared in the government of the realm in a remarkable way. Indeed, as Bindoff puts it, it was "the twenty or thirty men sitting at the hub of affairs in the Council or Star Chamber, and the six or seven hundred JPs covering the country…who were, at their respective levels, the chief agents of royal power in the early Tudor State."

What role if any did Parliament play in this early Tudor system of government? Maitland reminds us that, long before the reign of Henry VII, Parliament "had taken the shape familiar to us, an assembly consisting of two houses which sit, debate, and vote apart—the one containing the lords spiritual and temporal, the other all the representatives of the commons." Each house, like our Senate and House of Representatives, had also begun to meet in separate buildings, and both increasingly, like the modern Parliament, met in Westminster.[31]

Our Constitution specifies that "Congress shall assemble at least once in every year." Throughout the Middle Ages, it was "for the king to decide when and whether he would summon a parliament," but after the Model Parliament of 1295, "parliaments soon became very frequent." By 1330, a statute calls for annual parliaments. The frequency of meetings of Parliament was guaranteed by the king's need for money, as it was accepted that consent of king, lords, and commons was necessary for taxation. Parliament kept the king on a short leash, seldom voting permanent taxes, thus making the calling of annual parliaments "a practical necessity."

Article I of the U.S. Constitution also specifies that "all Bills for raising Revenue shall originate in the House of Representatives." As early as 1400, English kings had agreed that "money grants are to be initiated in the House of Commons"—a long step, as Maitland puts it, "towards that exclusive control over taxation which the House of Commons claimed in later ages."

This increasing financial power of Parliament in general and of the House of Commons in particular might seem to have put an effective limit on the power of the Tudor kings, until one recalls that Henry VII had made himself and his court independently rich by pressing to the utmost his claims for fines and reliefs from the nobility. Unlike his "habitually poor" royal predecessors, he could therefore call Parliament much less frequently. Maitland tells us that he "held but seven parliaments during his 24 years" on the throne.[32] Bindoff adds that, under Henry, "parliament was an institution which...existed only intermittently.... Henry availed himself of parliament when he had a use for it, and ignored it when he had not."[33]

When Henry VII called parliaments, they "did no more than he asked them to do." As Bindoff remarks, parliaments "forged the legislative weapons which he needed and, that being done, they dispersed again."[34] Maitland adds the amazing irony that these parliaments "are so pliant to the king's will that the king is very willing to acquiesce in every claim that parliament may make to be part of the sovereign body of the realm." From now on, a statute is "the king's act, done with the assent (sometimes the form runs 'advice and consent') of the lords spiritual and temporal and commons in parliament assembled and by the authority of the said parliament." By the Tudor era, the "statute book is already a hefty volume," as "king and parliament have taken upon themselves" to regulate every aspect of life.

Henry VII was, as Bindoff summarizes, "incomparably the best business man to sit upon the English throne."[35] When he died, he left his surviving younger son a large fortune, together with "the traditional organs of government, revitalized and in good working order." The ultimate positivist, a king who simply said he was king and acted accordingly, Henry leveled every medieval vestige except that of the Church. This "crowning acquisition...he left to the abundant energies of his successor,"[36] perhaps the most famous king in English history, Henry VIII.

TWELVE

Henry VIII, Thomas Cromwell, and the Tudor Constitutional Revolution

merican presidents have often been inferior to their immediate great predecessors. Martin Van Buren was no Andrew
Jackson; Andrew Johnson, no Abraham Lincoln; William
Howard Taft, no Theodore Roosevelt. Much the same at first seemed
to be true of Henry VII's heir. White reminds us that Henry VIII
"inherited not a tithe of his father's business sense...[or] appetite for
hard work."[1] Bindoff describes the contrast between father and son:

> The thirty-four years difference in age between the two Henrys
> who on 21 April 1509 were both King of England was the dif-
> ference between a wizened and toothless old man and a hand-
> some and lusty young one....Henry VII...starting from next
> to nothing, had built up a great family business, but [his] head
> remained conspicuously unturned...by success. Henry VIII,
> inheriting a flourishing concern, was to display traits charac-
> teristic of second generations. He spurned the drudgery of the
> office-stool and aspired to cut a figure in the world.[2]

The young Henry VIII seemed a true Renaissance king—tall, hand-
some, intelligent, and well educated enough to be able to "exchange
learned little Latin notes with Erasmus at the dinner table and compose music." He was not yet the fat, arrogant tyrant he would become.[3]

Different personalities of American presidents have produced different styles of governing. The same was true of Henry VII and his successor. "Clear headed and hardworking," Henry VII "presided with businesslike efficiency over his own Council."[4] Henry VIII was interested mainly in "girls and hunting," and he preferred to leave affairs of state to his chief minister.

Historians have long marveled at the meteoric rise of Henry's first minister, Thomas Wolsey, whom White calls "the last ecclesiastical statesman of the English Middle Ages." A butcher's son, he became "the king's right hand man, . . . one of the wealthiest and certainly the most powerful of the King's subjects."[5]

In *Kissinger's War*, Henry Paolucci tells us how Henry Kissinger rose from his career as Harvard professor to court minister when Richard Nixon appointed him as his national security adviser in 1969, and how Kissinger soon came to dominate every aspect of the Nixon White House. Like Kissinger, Wolsey soon drew "all legal business within his orbit." Kissinger made the State Department essentially irrelevant, channeling all foreign policy decisions through himself. Wolsey "virtually destroyed the inner ring of the council by concentrating its powers in himself." As in the case of the Nixon White House, Henry's councilors "rarely knew what went on until the cardinal deigned to inform them."

Wolsey also revived the chancellor's courts, particularly Star Chamber, which increased in authority so much under him that some "thought him the inventor of that court." Under Wolsey, Star Chamber encroached on the common law courts and became "part of the regular system of law-administration in England."[6]

Kissinger is not the only modern statesman whose control of government can be compared to that of Wolsey. Bindoff offers another useful comparison: "Wolsey . . . [was] similar to . . . Metternich . . . in the Austrian, or Bismarck in the German Empire. He concentrated political power . . . to a degree without parallel in English history, and his biography . . . [is] a history of England from 1512 to 1529."[7] G. R. Elton agrees. From 1515 to 1529, it was Wolsey, he says, who ruled England.[8]

Henry might have remained satisfied with his all-powerful minister. But, of course, Henry VIII had a problem. His wife Katherine could not bear him a son. He had a daughter, Mary, but every son Katherine had borne him had died in infancy. No son meant no heir, and "a king without an heir portended a kingdom without a king, and without a king the kingdom would surely perish."[9]

Of course, there was a solution: have the pope dissolve the marriage. But Katherine was Henry's brother's widow, so Henry had gotten a papal dispensation to marry her in the first place. Now Henry was asking his chancellor to get the pope to dispense with the dispensation. Moreover, Rome was then in the control of Charles V of Spain. The pope dared not offend him, and Charles was Katherine's nephew.

"Out of this deadlock," one historian aptly notes, "grew the English Reformation."[10] To gain some perspective on the immense consequences on constitutional development that this change portended, one must consider the relationship of church, state, and law in England at the time.

Until the Tudors, the religious organization of England had followed the pattern of all Western Europe. Prior to the Reformation, Christianity was uniform. One system of church law—canon law— emanated from Rome and ruled this church.

There were, however, special differences in the English church-state situation. England had developed a unity of law and administration earlier than most of the other nations of Europe. Because of the power and prestige of the kings, there was no papal supremacy of temporal affairs in England. Moreover, there had long been a fairly high degree of anticlericalism. Many Englishmen "thought little of priests."[11] Some of Chaucer's most brilliant lines poke fun at the church. Most of all, there was resentment of the law that gave the clergy privileges which others did not enjoy—such as the right to be tried by an ecclesiastical court and subject to lesser punishment than would otherwise be inflicted.

We have seen how these privileges led to the bitter quarrel between Henry II and Thomas Becket. Over time, these privileges—or "benefit of clergy"—"had been stretched to cover almost anyone who could read." Henry VII had stopped this expansion of the privilege, limiting it to true clergy. But his statutory reform "tended to reduce the size of the problem...at the cost of re-emphasizing its ecclesiastical character."[12] Benefit of clergy was seen as one of the scandals of the church, especially in the south and east of England, which was closest to the continent.

It was, after all, on the continent that the Reformation was being born. It had started in Germany with Martin Luther in 1517. At first, the Tudors protected the church in England from Lutheranism. Heretics were denounced; Luther's books, burned. Henry VIII wrote a defense of the pope against Luther, for which he was given the title Defender of the Faith.

But Henry's choice of Wolsey for chancellor did not help rein in the public demand for church reformation. On the contrary, as White puts it, it was Wolsey who "probably did more than any other single figure to create the English anti-clerical neurosis which was to remain for so long a powerful and constant feature of the national character."[13] Elton reminds us that this great Cardinal "put Church reform at the bottom of his long list of preoccupations."[14] Wolsey's appetite for lavish palaces and ostentatious vulgarity gave the church an even worse reputation than it already had in England. Little else could hardly be expected from a man of the cloth who would go to court "holding to his nose an orange stuffed with a sponge steeped in vinegar" to protect him against the stench of the masses.[15]

In the end, it was not Wolsey's decadence that brought him down but his failure to please his king. Every all-powerful minister is only strong as long as he remains in favor with his chief. Bismarck fell from power when a new German kaiser felt no need of him; Kissinger finally departed when a new president, Jimmy Carter, replaced Kissinger's former boss Gerald Ford. In Wolsey's case, he failed to secure the king's divorce. Henry charged him with praemunire, a legal term for "the whole complex of laws limiting papal encroachments on the king's 'crown and regality.' "[16] Before Wolsey could be sent to the Tower, he fell gravely ill. In the film *A Man for All Seasons*, we see Wolsey (portrayed by Orson Welles) on his deathbed, saying, "If I had served God half as well as I served my king, he would not have left me to die in this place." Wolsey died in disgrace, and Henry appointed Thomas More, the great humanist and man of letters, as his new chancellor.

Thomas More is the patron saint of lawyers. Called to the bar after study at Lincoln's Inn, he had been brilliantly successful. But More was also a man of God, and when he became chancellor, he asked the king to leave him out of the matter of the divorce.

The king tried to get the divorce on his own and didn't do it very well, asking lawmakers to put pressure on the church. Parliament was only too happy to oblige. As Elton says, the Commons "was representative of...[those] who were particularly hostile to the pretensions and exactions of the Church."[17] Hitherto the king had "stood between the Church and its lay enemies; now, that protector cheered on the hunt."[18]

At first, the revolution took place in stages. Individual members of the clergy were indicted. Then the whole clergy was forced to surrender to the king's will by being charged with praemunire.

In 1532, More resigned the chancellorship and for a time lived in retirement. But when he refused to swear an oath that would impugn the pope's authority, he was committed to the Tower of London. Tried for high treason, More defended himself by invoking natural law: "And forasmuch as this Indictment is grounded upon an Act of Parliament directly repugnant to the laws of God and His Holy Church... it is therefore in law...insufficient to charge any Christian man."[19]

More was found guilty and beheaded in 1535. By then, a new minister had been appointed to the king's council—another Thomas, Thomas Cromwell. This was the true beginning of the Tudor Revolution.

Cromwell's significance for the future course of Anglo-American constitutionalism can hardly be exaggerated. He was, as Elton says, "the most remarkable revolutionary in English history—a man who knew precisely where he was going and who nearly always achieved the end he had in view."[20] It was he who "founded the modern constitutional monarchy in England and organized the sovereign national state."[21]

Men of his time knew him only as the "all-powerful minister." But his fame and reputation suffered a great deal after his death. Historians tried to restore Henry's reputation by putting the blame for the English Reformation on Cromwell. They called him Machiavellian. Although he certainly was Machiavellian, he was also a great statecrafter—England's greatest. Classical scholar Henry Paolucci explains Cromwell's legacy in his *Brief History of Political Thought and Statecraft*: "Thomas Cromwell has gone down in history, like Machiavelli, as a great villain. But he is, in fact, the villain who, virtually alone, with his Machiavellian statecraft, made possible the glorious Elizabethan age of England that gave us Edmund Spenser, Shakespeare, and Sir Francis Bacon."[22]

Cromwell was far better situated than his predecessor to succeed in the divorce. "Completely secular-minded, . . . [with] little or no respect for clergymen,"[23] he had a simple solution to Henry's problem: evict the pope from England. Henry saw this as the way to get his divorce. Cromwell saw it as the way to reconstruct the whole body politic.

The point, however, is that he accomplished this revolution through law. Starting in 1531, Cromwell got Parliament to pass laws, weakening the Papacy's control of the church in England. The Act of Appeals put all ecclesiastical jurisdiction under the king, specifying that "henceforth in spiritual suits, appeals should lie, not to Rome, but to the Archbishop of Canterbury" and thus ultimately to the king. This act begins with a famous preamble: "This realm of England is an empire . . . governed by one supreme Head and King."[24] England for the first time declared itself to be a sovereign state—free and independent of foreign authority. This was the English Declaration of Independence.

In time, we get also the Act of Supremacy, which declared the king to be "Supreme Head of the Church of England."[25] Along with all this, of course, came the famous dissolution of the monasteries and the start of "one of the most miserable periods of English history."[26] Cromwell wanted church property, for the crown's finances were far from healthy. So, church property was taken. Buildings were destroyed; great works of art, ruined. The really surprising thing in all this is not that it happened, but that it happened so easily.

It was Cromwell who made it happen so easily. As Elton explains, he carried out this revolution "with the consent of the politically conscious and active classes, and with an almost finicky attention to constitutional propriety." From the perspective of the later development of American law, Cromwell set a precedent that would be used by presidents from Wilson to George W. Bush in seeking congressional authorization for executive powers.

The essence of Cromwell's revolution was national sovereignty. Elton explains that the crucial word in the preamble to the Act of Appeals is "empire": "This realm of England is an Empire, ... governed by one Supreme Head and King." Earlier kings had often called themselves emperors because they ruled more than one state, some claiming to rule Scotland; others, France. "In the act of appeals, on the other hand, England by herself is described as an empire, and ... the word here denoted a political unit, a self-governing state. ... We call this sort of thing a sovereign national state." Elton goes on to illuminate the constitutional point: "England is an independent state, sovereign within its territorial limits. It is governed by a ruler who is both supreme head in matters spiritual and king in matters temporal, and who possesses ... 'plenary, whole, and entire power, preeminence, authority, prerogative, and jurisdiction to render and yield justice' to all people and subjects resident within his realm."[27]

We think of the king's supremacy over the church as the chief legacy of the Tudor Revolution. But Elton is right to say that "this is so only because the principle of national sovereignty was established in a struggle with the ecclesiastical authority of Rome; ... The principle, which is much more important than the particular application, is the same: absence of outside authority, ... national sovereignty."[28]

It is tempting to see in this the seeds of divine-right tyranny and to regard the Tudor era as a deviation from the tradition of representative government that we have today. Nothing could be further from the truth, however. Cromwell's "deliberate decision to take the nation 'into partnership' was the most momentous step in the rise of Parliament." Elton explains why: "Until Parliament has decreed that certain activities...are criminal,...there is no way in which the supremacy can be enforced....Parliament thus legalized the Reformation...in the severely practical sense of making possible the prosecution...of those who opposed the royal policy."[29]

According to Elton, Cromwell's Henrician Reformation thus laid the foundation for a central tenet of American constitutionalism—the supremacy of law. As Elton explains, it made clear that there was to be "no thought—no possibility—of a purely royal despotism." On the other hand, what Cromwell applied differs from the rule of law we Americans know. In our system, the Constitution is the supreme law, and courts can declare statutes unconstitutional. By contrast, according to "Reformation statutes demonstrate that the political sovereignty...was to be a parliamentary one....The highest authority in the land was recognized to lie in that assembly of king, lords, and commons....The Tudor revolution established the supremacy and omnicompetence of statute...[and said] that there was no sphere of life closed to it—that it could do what it wished."

Elton goes on to say that, at the time, perhaps only two men in all of England understood the significance of what was happening:

> Thomas Cromwell certainly knew what he was doing....[He was] well aware of the supreme importance of statute and parliament in the revolution. The other man was Thomas More who declared that he could not obey an act of Parliament when it went contrary to the law of Christendom. In this More represented the conception of a universal Christian law to which man-made law must conform....But however right More may have been in abstract philosophy and as a member of a Christian

community, as a subject of King Henry VIII and his laws he was utterly wrong. When Cromwell, the first statesman to understand the potentialities of statute, used it to enforce great revolutionary changes through the courts of law, he demonstrated that in law and on earth, there is nothing that an act of parliament cannot do.[30]

This triumph of Parliament did not mean a weakening of the common law. Rather, Cromwell's policy strengthened the common law where his predecessor Wolsey had tried to weaken it. Elton tells us that Cromwell "has been falsely accused of wishing to introduce the Roman law in England." Actually, it was Henry VIII, under the influence of Wolsey and Cardinal Pole, who had seriously contemplated a complete discarding of the common law and a Romanization of the law of England. It was Cromwell's leadership that saved Henry's England from this Romanization—and thus saved the common law from royal absolutism. Acting through Parliament and through law, Cromwell thus gave England a new sovereignty. As Elton says, when "Cromwell died, the state and kingship of England were very different from what they had been at the fall of Wolsey." Henry Paolucci elaborates:

Thomas Cromwell did some terrible things to make England great, and he paid for it dearly, with his head. Nevertheless, he deserves to be ranked as England's greatest political thinker in the practical sense, as well as its greatest statesman.... Cromwell made possible a continued growth of the form of parliamentary-monarchic government—of government of the King in Parliament—that had ruled England since the end of the thirteenth century. This he achieved by inducing King Henry VIII not only to separate himself from Rome—to make England fully free—but also to do it with the approval of Parliament and in Parliament. That Parliament was then a rubber-stamp institution. Henry could have done without its approval. But Cromwell, looking ahead to a time when kings could no longer claim divine right, made provision for the future. He saw to it that, if ever an English king had to give up divine right claims, a Parliament speaking for the people would be at hand with long-established precedents.[31]

Before he fell out of favor and lost his head, Cromwell got Parliament to make Henry head of the Church of England. Henry's own church gave him the divorce he wanted, marrying him to Anne Boleyn. Henry then tired of Anne, too, and had her beheaded for treason. He eventually went through four more wives, all of whom were either divorced or beheaded or both (except the last, who survived him).

By Henry's death in 1547, England was a different place: The king was head of the church. England was a sovereign nation state. The king in Parliament—king, lords, and Commons—was absolutely supreme.

Henry VIII's reign was followed by a period of religious extremism, in which the country, freed from the Papacy, lurched ominously from one religious side to the other—first Protestantism under Edward VI when churches were pilloried and sacred images were smashed, and then Catholicism under Mary, known as Bloody Mary because she had so many Protestants burned at the stake. Finally, in 1558, Henry VIII was succeeded by a daughter who truly made England great and preserved the nation-building that her father had started. That great daughter, of course, was Elizabeth.

In foreign policy, Elizabeth proved a statesman of great skill, defeating Spain's Armada in the famous year of 1588 and thereby ushering in the age of Shakespeare and a new spirit of nationalism. On the religious issue, Elizabeth's greatness was that she did not accentuate the church problem—she muted it. Avoiding both extremes, Catholicism and Puritanism, she succeeded in not offending the great bulk of moderate religious opinion.

When Elizabeth died, childless, in 1603, England was left with an impressive Tudor legacy. To visualize the Tudor achievements, it is perhaps best to recall that in 1485, when Elizabeth's grandfather

Henry VII, the first Tudor, took the throne, England was, as R. J. White puts it, "'a small rough spot on the rim of sixteenth-century Europe,' veritably 'little England,' a green island off the coast of the continent, much as Ireland was for long to be 'the other island' of John Bull." Wales had been annexed, but Scotland was still as separate a kingdom as France. Moreover, even within the confines of the small island, there was little legal unity. There were, as White says, "extensive regions where the king's writ ran but lamely, franchises...where the word of a bishop was better heeded than the word of the king's justices." Communication between regions was scarcely better than in the time of the Romans, so that rebellions "almost anywhere had at least a twenty-four hours' start" before they could be suppressed. Large areas of the country were still "clad in forest, and many thousands of acres suppressed in marsh and fen." In short, England was "no sun but a satellite." Rulers of France and Spain "made passes at England" and regarded her much as the Romans had done in ancient times—as "an off-shore base to be taken into custody sooner or later, as strategy or trade requirements would determine."

Even then, of course, England had potential. Her coasts looked both east and west, "to the markets of the Low Countries, the Baltic, and the great transatlantic unknown." Her common law system of representative government needed only "the aggressive energies and intelligence of a masterful monarchy" to be revived. "Within a century," White concludes, the Tudors had completed that revival and "set the English on the road to their modern destiny."[32] William McElwee elaborates: "They had broken feudalism, completed a religious reformation without civil war, and fought off the most serious external threat England had faced since the Conquest,...without...weakening England's fundamental laws and liberties....The ultimate sovereign was the King in Parliament."[33]

This new sovereignty worked well for England and English law as long as the interests of Crown and Commons remained more or less identical, as in the Tudor age. But Elizabeth's death left England with problems that would soon lead to differences "over which a more self-confident and businesslike House of Commons would begin to assert its own point of view."

Although Elizabeth had defeated Philip of Spain's Armada, England, with no more foreign rival to unite against, felt domestic religious tensions begin to reerupt—just as Rome's defeat of Carthage had paved the way for civil war at home, much as Polybius had foreseen. Puritanism was spreading among the more educated classes that dominated the House of Commons, and, even in the later years of Elizabeth's reign, the House began to challenge the Crown in matters of religion. Elizabeth at first prohibited all discussion of religion and punished disobedience with imprisonment, sending some of the more outspoken members of Parliament to the Tower. But in the end, even she had to allow the Commons to debate specific points of "Ecclesiastical Reformation."[34]

England's economy was still based on one crop: wool. When the wool industry did badly, the whole country went into economic decline. No institution felt this financial pinch more than the monarchy. Under Henry, and later under Elizabeth, the monarchs had been accustomed to asking Parliament for money, and so the constitutional custom that only Parliament could tax had been strengthened.

Parliament had survived Henry's Reformation because of Thomas Cromwell's reliance on Parliament for legislation and getting money. It was this power over the purse that made Parliament strong, and it continued to be strong under Elizabeth. She convened Parliament frequently, and by her death it seemed inevitable to everyone that Parliament was there to stay and that it had the sole authority to tax and raise revenue.

Such a strong Parliament could work well with a Tudor monarch like Henry VIII or his daughter Elizabeth if for no other reason than because of their extraordinary political genius. Historian White reminds us that this was the greatest gift of the Tudors. "This astounding family of kings and queens had a genius for politics,... for wanting generally what their people wanted [and] for self-preservation. Heretics (except Mary) in an overwhelmingly Catholic world, they all died in their beds, except Elizabeth, [but only because she] preferred to die on the floor, propped up on cushions."[35]

Having given us a sense of this remarkable Tudor political skill, White then adds a keen description of one last and perhaps most important Tudor weakness: "The one failure of the Tudor family was in the matter of begetting healthy male heirs. Not one of them succeeded in this elementary task after Henry VII, whereas the House of Stuart bred men children regularly, to their own and every one else's misfortune. It was as if, having produced the miracle of the Tudor genius, nature broke the mould. It was, perhaps, too rare for mass production."[36]

This Tudor failure to produce male heirs, as we have seen, precipitated the Henrician Reformation. Similarly, Elizabeth's death with no heir at all forced the English to turn to another dynasty, the Stuarts. We now turn to the enormous consequences for law and constitutionalism which that unhappy family produced.

THIRTEEN

James I and the Start of the English Constitutional Crisis of the Seventeenth Century

In his book *Stuart England*, J. P. Kenyon reminds us of the Whig version of seventeenth-century English history:

> Disaster at once became inevitable when that remarkable woman Queen Elizabeth... [was succeeded by] the feckless and incompetent Stuarts, who... tried to establish an un-English despotism based on... the Divine Right of Kings.... [Eventually, they were] painlessly removed by... the Whigs... [whose] form of government proceeded... down to the present day, and which not only made the nation Free and Rich but showed it to be Great and Right.[1]

Kenyon, like most other modern historians, is sharply critical of this "theory of inevitable, predestined, almost effortless parliamentary advance." He points out that, to an Englishman living in the 1600s, the opposite result would have seemed far more likely. On the continent of Europe, "princely power was waxing," and the power of assemblies and parliaments was "waning or disappearing altogether."[2] It would have seemed far more natural that the English king would end up being the absolute sovereign and Parliament eventually a ceremonial figurehead rather than the other way around.

How then did England once again resist the trend in which all of Europe was moving? This is an extremely important question for our study of the background of American constitutionalism because it was in this same seventeenth century that England embraced the tradition of limited constitutional government that is our heritage. It is true that the origins of all the important institutions of the English government predated the Stuarts: the monarchy, council, courts of law and equity, even Parliament itself had all been in place for hundreds of years by the time James I succeeded Elizabeth. Still, the peculiar English and ultimately American balance of legislative, executive, and judicial powers takes shape in this vitally important century. When the seventeenth century began, England's monarch could still claim a divine right to rule. By century's end, he or she could not. The tradition of what Locke and Jefferson called government by consent had been born. How did this change come about and with what consequences for America?

In considering this century of change, we must remember that, although the events and ideas of seventeenth-century England contributed greatly to our modern understanding of constitutional government, for most men the debate at the time was not framed in those terms. If you had asked an Englishman why he opposed James I in 1610 or why he was fighting against Charles I in the English Civil War in 1645, he would not have replied that he was fighting to secure the sovereignty of Parliament and constitutional democracy. If he put the issue in grand political terms at all, he would have said only that the king had too much power.

Power is a word that Thomas Hobbes introduced into the vocabulary of modern political science. As Kenyon reminds us, the whole debate of seventeenth-century England was about power—about "physical authority, the ability to command men's obedience." The issue was the same one that has dominated so much of history—who should rule? In this case, the two options were the king on the one hand and Parliament on the other. Elaborate theoretical ideas of constitutional government were far from the minds of all but the most abstract philosophers. Nor did people see what they were doing as setting the precedent for government by consent. They were enmeshed in the vital struggles of the moment, concerned with what was happening at the time.

Moreover, although English history in the 1600s generated ideas that had a huge impact on American constitutional development—such as judicial review and equality before the law—many of these experiments were rejected in England by century's end. Some ideas, such as democracy, were postponed in England, as indeed they would be in America as well. Others, such as judicial review, never caught on in England at all, although they did here. In some respects, then, seventeenth-century English history influenced America more than it did England herself.

James I and His Battle with Parliament and the Common Law Courts

In his *Constitutional History of England*, Maitland elaborates a number of important parliamentary privileges, all of which were more fully developed during the reign of James I, and all of which have direct correspondents in our Constitution.

Article I of our Constitution specifies that "for any Speech or Debate in either House, [members of Congress] shall not be questioned in any other place." Maitland tells us of the medieval origins of the right of each house of Parliament to debate freely without interference from the king. Reviewing Elizabeth's quarrels with Parliament, he speaks of the Protestation of 1621 in which the House of Commons boldly told the king that Parliament could debate any subject.

Article I, Section 6 also specifies that members of Congress shall "be privileged from Arrest during their Attendance at the Session of their respective Houses, and in going to and returning from the same." Maitland tells us that, during the reign of James I, "the representatives of the commons seem to have claimed a similar liberty [from arrest] during the session of parliament and for a certain time before and after the session reasonably necessary for their coming and going."

Maitland also mentions the power of each house "to punish persons (whether they be members of it or not) for a contempt." Our own Congress has such quasi-judicial powers, too. President Nixon risked being held "in contempt of Congress" when he disobeyed lower federal court orders to turn over the Watergate tapes.

Maitland calls impeachment "a weapon of enormous importance." Its more frequent use during the Stuart era, he says, contrasts with the earlier Tudor years when Bills of Attainder were more often used to destroy opponents of the Crown. Our Constitution also makes this distinction. The House of Representatives is explicitly given the "sole Power of Impeachment." By contrast, Bills of Attainder, seen by the framers as legislative punishment without trial, are forbidden, both for the state legislatures and Congress.

By James I's death, Maitland adds, the "function of originating money bills" is clearly "among the privileges of the House of Commons." Our Constitution states that all "Bills for raising Revenue shall originate in the House of Representatives," our equivalent of the House of Commons. Maitland also mentions that, during James I's reign, the Commons claimed "a right to determine all questions relating to the election of members of their house." Our Constitution specifies that each "House shall be the Judge of the Elections, Returns, and Qualifications of its own members."

Before the Stuarts, Parliament was still an occasionally summoned assembly. Kenyon notes that, although "Elizabeth's financial needs...caused her to meet Parliament with increasing frequency,...these were all separate parliaments and their sessions were brief; men still spoke of 'this parliament,' or 'the parliaments,' not of 'Parliament' in general."[3] This changed under James I. By the mid-1600s, England is recognizing Parliament as a "permanent entity, in which the sovereignty of the realm might be vested."[4] The framers of our Constitution, mindful of the Stuarts' attempts to destroy that permanence, clarified that Congress must "assemble at least once in every Year."

With an eye to that change, Maitland describes the parliaments of Henry VIII as "submissive"; those of Elizabeth, "grumble"; while "parliaments of James I more than once resist him and defeat him." Kenyon also notes that it "was the breakdown of this general cooperation" between monarch and Parliament that led to "The Winning of the Initiative by the House of Commons."[5] This breakdown is the crucial link in understanding the genesis of British and American legislative power. How did the trust that had existed between the Tudor monarchs and their parliaments disappear in the Stuart years, and how did events culminate in an open civil war between king and Parliament?

The idea of civil war could not have been further from the minds of the English in 1603 when Elizabeth's successor, the first Stuart, took the throne. In fact, England in 1603 was a comparatively quiet place. As the *Oxford History of Britain* puts it, there were more dead bodies on the stage at the end of a production of *Hamlet* than there were in battlefields of England in the first forty years of the seventeenth century.

Moreover, James, who came to the throne in the first thoroughly peaceful succession in nearly a century, was at first welcomed by his subjects as a "learned and literary ruler" who had "already shown himself a seasoned and eminently successful" monarch.[6] As Roy Strong puts it in his *Story of Britain*, James "had been king of Scotland almost from birth and had learnt his statecraft in the rugged school of Scottish politics."[7]

From the start, however, James had weaknesses. Accustomed to working with a small Scottish Parliament, he "was frustrated by [an English Parliament] which was too large for him to negotiate with face to face ... except through ... public speeches."[8] He made a bad impression when he spoke. He had a foreign (Scottish) accent and appeared to be exactly what he was—lazy, boring, and vain. Most important, people did not like what he had to say in his speeches about his divine right to rule: "The state of monarchy is the supremest thing upon earth; for kings are not only God's lieutenants upon earth, ... but even by God himself they are called gods.... [Just] as to dispute what God may do is blasphemy, ... so is it sedition in subjects to dispute what a king may do in the height of his power."[9]

No president of the United States could make such a statement today, or have a painter like Reubens depict a scene of his glorious ascension into heaven on the ceiling of one of his great halls, as the Stuart monarchs did.[10] Presidents are expected to be always in the public eye. By contrast, probably not more than one in a thousand Englishmen ever saw James I. Moreover, he "was not the king men were looking for in the early seventeenth century."[11] Goldwin Smith remarks that history could have been quite different: "Had the first Stuart been more a practical man of action than of words, ... the royal will might have been blunted early enough to have prevented the crisis that was to cost Charles I his life. But the chief interests of James I were ... searching out of witches and 'counterfeit wenches,' and the parading of his ideas of kingcraft and prerogative."[12]

To be fair to James, his money problem was in some measure an inherited one, like the problems that American presidents sometimes inherit from their predecessors. Elizabeth left a large debt, and the costs of her funeral and James's coronation were staggering. In 1603, when England plunged into depression, "no one felt the pinch more than the Crown."

In 2014, with its huge deficit, America seems to need fiscal restraint, and yet our government is amassing bigger and bigger deficits. The same was true of England under James. Instead of frugality, he met the financial crisis with more lavish spending. Coupled with his extravagance at home, his ambitious plans for colonization in Ireland and the New World meant that he had to have more money. Then, however, the king was still expected to live "of his own," from his revenues from Crown lands and other feudal dues, asking for money from Parliament only for war. Increasingly, James found that he needed more revenue all the time. There were but two solutions: Parliament could tax regularly even in peacetime or the king could dismiss Parliament and collect money from people directly.

On the continent, the second alternative was the accepted one.

In England, however, a long tradition that taxes must be authorized by statute had already developed. So James went, hat in hand, to his Parliament. It is probably not surprising that the reception he got was anything but enthusiastic. As Kenyon puts it, "there was never very much likelihood that James would be treated by Parliament with the same generosity as Elizabeth, especially since he needed larger sums than she did without the excuse of a war emergency." If kings really were God's lieutenants on earth, Parliament argued, "they should model their lives on His," and observe the Christian virtue of frugality.[13] As Goldwin Smith reminds us, Parliament's attitude toward the monarchy had changed: "There was a wide gap between the kind of world Henry VII had found in 1485 and that left by the passing of the great Queen in 1603.... The house of commons was ready to win the initiative in the face of Stuart obstruction and incompetence."[14]

After prolonged debate, James "granted the right of the house of commons to be...judge of returns of its own members," but in doing so he insisted that "all the 'privileges' of the commons resulted from an act of grace on his part." They were not natural or historic rights but favors granted temporarily by the king.[15]

Parliament would brook no such arrogance. Declaring "the voice of the people...the voice of God," they protested that "the privileges of parliament are the ancient and undoubted birthright of the subjects of England." James was so angry that he sent for the journal of the Commons and literally tore out this protest using his own hands.[16] In Parliament today, one can still see this journal, with the torn page clearly evident.

Disputes like these led to an impasse over finances, as battles between the president and Congress often do in America today. Parliament's unwillingness to tax to support the king's spending led him to turn to his own sources of revenue—special taxes and requisitions— and to his prerogative courts to enforce them. This put him in conflict with the common law courts, and with one common law judge in particular, Sir Edward Coke.

Attorney general under Elizabeth and later chief justice of

Common Pleas, Coke came to believe that the king's prerogative courts were wrongfully encroaching on the jurisdiction of common law courts and began issuing "prohibitions," "written orders...forbidding other courts to hear particular matters." The king took offense and summoned Coke to explain himself. As reported by Coke, the king's position was that he "may take what Causes he shall please to determine from the Determination of the Judges, and may determine them himself." Coke replied "that the King in his own Person cannot adjudge any case" because "the judgments are always given per curiam ['by the court'] and the Judges...are sworn to execute Justice according to Law and Customs of England." The king apparently then told Coke that it was his understanding that "Law was founded upon Reason, and that he and others had Reason, as well as the Judges." Yes, Coke boldly replied, "but his majesty was not learned in the Laws of his Realm of England" nor trained in "the artificial Reason and Judgment of Law,...an Art which requires long Study and Experience, before that a man can attain to the cognizance of it." The king was greatly offended by this. Coke answered by quoting Bracton: "The King is not under any man, but is under God and the law."[17]

Maitland tells us that Coke was later elevated to the position of chief justice of King's Bench, "seemingly in the hope that in a more exalted position he would prove more pliant."[18] It didn't work. Coke continued to challenge the king. In one particularly rough personal encounter, Coke "fell 'flat on all fours' as James threatened to strike him, 'looking and speaking fiercely with bended fist.' "[19] Eventually, Coke was dismissed. By 1620, he had taken a seat in Parliament, "and from that time until his death in 1634, [he] did not a little to give the great struggle its peculiar character, a struggle of the common law against the king."[20]

The theory behind Coke's actions illustrates the American significance of this struggle. Coke saw the common law as controlling both king and Parliament. In Dr. Bonham's Case in 1610, Coke declared that "when an act of Parliament is against common right or reason, or repugnant or impossible to be performed, the common law will control it and adjudge such act to be void." Some legal historians assert that this is an early anticipation of the American doctrine of judicial review, the power of judges to declare acts of legislatures unconstitutional. Others insist it is not. Undeniably, however, in America, ideas like those of Coke developed into judicial review, whereas in England parliamentary supremacy won and judicial review died unborn.

In the end, the supremacy of Parliament was won; therefore the idea of a fundamental law broke off short in England. In the American colonies, the idea was taken up in the eighteenth century. The governmental structure of the United States, including the system of judicial review, would have been more intelligible to Sir Edward Coke than the idea of the sovereignty of Parliament.[21]

This supremacy of Parliament was, of course, still a long way off when James battled with his Parliament. By the end of his reign, that battle was beginning to take on all the characteristics of a furious fight between the president and Congress in our system. Most dangerous to the king were the Puritans, "those left wing Protestants within the Church of England who wanted less ritual." James, who had also antagonized Catholics with his cruel reaction to the Gunpowder Plot, told the Puritans to conform to his Anglican Church or he would "harry them out of the land," thus inspiring many of them to flee to New England and bring with them many radical notions that a turbulent age of "dizzying changes of mood and outbursts of violent emotion" was generating.[22]

When James I died in 1625, his legacy was at best a mixed one. Halliday reminds us that James's reign "saw the publication of the Authorized Version of the Bible, perhaps the finest prose work in our language, the greatest plays of Shakespeare, from *Othello* to *The Tempest*, the first classical buildings in England, those of Inigo Jones, the beginnings of the British Empire and of English science" and Francis Bacon, who was "preparing the way for the exact experimental science of the new age."[23] On the debit side, however, James was not successful with Parliament. As her biographer Catherine Drinker Bowen has written, Elizabeth "flattered her Commons." James, by contrast, viewed parliaments as "'recurrent trials' laid on him."[24] Roy Strong says that "the ship of state may have become progressively leakier" under James, "but it just managed to remain on course. Under his successor, it was to sink amidst a sea of recriminations."[25] Maitland is more ominous: "Everywhere we see that the storm is coming."[26]

FOURTEEN

From Civil War to Glorious Revolution

In *The Imperial Presidency*, Arthur Schlesinger describes how presidents Lyndon Johnson and Richard Nixon became isolated from Congress and the country, surrounding themselves only with men who would tell them what they wanted to hear. The same can be said of Charles I. Historian Roy Strong says that while James I "had endured public appearances, Charles rarely if ever made them, his court becoming a closed world from which he excluded those whose views did not coincide with his own. The result was gradually to cut the monarchy adrift from any popular support."[1]

Also like some modern presidents, Charles faced a financial crisis of great magnitude. The country was still engaged in wars that it could not afford, and Charles, like his father and his twentieth- and twenty-first-century counterparts, turned to Parliament for money. From the beginning, however, Parliament was distrustful and uncooperative. The members feared Charles's high church doctrines were moving the country closer to Rome and disliked Charles's assertions about divine right. Instead of granting duties to the king for the life of the monarch, as was their wont, they granted them for one year only. Strong gives us a marvelous modern parallel relevant to conflicts from Vietnam to Iraq when he says that the "pattern began of parliaments refusing to pay for mishandled wars over the course of which they had no control." As in the case of Johnson and Nixon, the stage was set on both sides for "bitterness and recriminations leading to polarization."

To raise money, Charles sold off the last of the Crown lands, a move which "represented the effective end of medieval kingship, for when the lands went the king no longer had anything 'of his own' by which to pay for government." Faced with a recalcitrant Parliament that seemed to want government without paying for it, Charles raised money by "forced loans."

In 1775, America began a revolution because of "taxation without representation." Charles's forced loans 150 years earlier were, in effect, taxation without any legislative approval at all. Many openly refused to pay. When Charles arbitrarily imprisoned several of them, a "wise man remarked that 'the whole nation cannot be consigned to prison, your majesty.'"[2] Among those imprisoned were five knights, who immediately sought writs of habeas corpus from the Court of King's Bench.

Maitland describes the medieval origins of the writ of habeas corpus, a privilege later protected in Article I of our Constitution. As early as Henry II, when "anyone was imprisoned it was the king's power to inquire the cause of the imprisonment." On plea of the prisoner, "the king would send his writ [of habeas corpus, Latin for 'you have the body'] to the keeper of the gaol, bidding him have the body of that subject before the king's court." In time, "this prerogative of the king came to be regarded as the right of the subject." A prisoner "aggrieved by the refusal of the sheriff...to let him...[post bail] could by means of the writ of habeas corpus bring his case before one of the common law courts."[3]

This is precisely what was done in the Case of the Five Knights. The writs sought by the prisoners were granted by the Court of King's Bench, but "the warden of Fleet Prison refused to release the prisoners," declaring "he was acting...'by special order of His Majesty.'"[4]

A remarkably similar incident took place in 1861 during the American Civil War. After President Lincoln suspended the writ of habeas corpus in Baltimore, John Merryman, a Confederate sympathizer, was arrested, by General Cadwallader, and imprisoned. Hearing Merryman's petition, Chief Justice Roger Taney caused a writ of habeas corpus to be served, directing the general to produce 'the body' in court. Cadwallader's instructions [from the president] were to hold in secure confinement all persons implicated in treasonable practices and to decline for the time to produce prisoners where writs of habeas corpus were issued, by whatsoever authority. In the respectful return to the writ, he stated the cause for which Merryman was apprehended, cited the President's suspension as authority for the detention, and declined to obey the mandate. Taney then issued a writ of attachment for contempt against the general, but the marshall seeking to serve this writ was refused entrance to the fort and would have encountered superior force had he attempted...to compel the general's appearance.[5]

The Five Knights Case of 1627 and the Merryman case of 1861 thus presented the same important constitutional issue: "could the courts of common law bail [release] a prisoner who was imprisoned by the king's [or president's] commandment?"[6] In Merryman's case, Chief Justice Taney went on to write a famous opinion reprimanding Lincoln for suspending habeas corpus and asserting that only Congress could suspend that writ, an opinion that Lincoln just as famously ignored. In the Five Knights Case, however, the justices, not protected by the same independence of the judiciary that Taney and every federal judge in America enjoys, yielded to royal pressure and held that this was "presumed to be a matter of state which we cannot take notice of." There were no precedents, Chief Justice Hyde said, for releasing prisoners where reasons of state and the king's orders were involved. Like the U.S. Supreme Court in the Prize Cases, which upheld Lincoln's blockade of the South without congressional declaration of war, the justices in the Five Knights Case concluded that the "King hath done it, and we can trust him in great matters."[7]

The judges also yielded to the king in cases involving ship money. The Crown had imposed a levy on England's port towns to pay for the navy. Charles extended this tax to all counties of England and Wales.

Upholding this, a court ruled "the king had the right, absolute and unimpaired, to decide when there was a national emergency."[8] One can only imagine the consequences of a comparable decision about presidential power to declare emergency in America today.

With victories like those, Charles seemed to be gaining the upper hand. Like the American colonists in 1776, members of Parliament in 1628 decided to compile their grievances against Charles into a Petition of Right, a document that "ranks along with Magna Carta...in placing constitutional limits on absolute monarchy" and that insists that "no man hereafter be compelled to make or yield any [tax]...without common consent by act of parliament." Like our Bill of Rights, the Petition of Right condemned arbitrary imprisonment and compulsory billeting of troops. The Supreme Court in Ex Parte Milligan, after Lincoln's death, ruled that "martial rule can never exist where the courts are open." The Petition of Right similarly condemns martial rule as contrary to the spirit of the law.[9]

Like King John at Runnymede before him, Charles reluctantly accepted the Petition of Right. But when Parliament launched an attack on his chief minister, Buckingham, Charles, like a president whose attorney general is under investigation on Capitol Hill, refused to distinguish between attacks on himself and on his subordinates. The commons began impeachment proceedings against Buckingham for corruption and maladministration. When Buckingham was murdered in 1628, Charles, embittered and alone—like Lyndon Johnson after the Tet Offensive or Richard Nixon after the Saturday Night Massacre—began openly ignoring the Petition of Right and adjourned Parliament. The ensuing scene was a dramatic one: "The obstreperous house of commons...voted against adjourning. When the Speaker tried to comply with the royal order he was seized and held in his chair. The doors were locked.... [Resolutions condemning royal tyranny were passed.]...Then the doors were unlocked, and the royal messengers were admitted,...and Parliament was dissolved."[10]

Charles said that he "'abhorred the very name of Parliament'" and that he would "govern by those means God put into my hands." For eleven years, he did.

Because of our constitutional requirement that Congress meet at least once a year and, even more, because we have come to regard Congress as a perpetual institution, it is difficult for us to imagine how Charles could have ruled without Parliament for eleven years, much less how there was a real threat then that Parliament would disappear altogether. On the continent, representative institutions such as Parliament were disappearing right and left as rulers inevitably found they could run their governments more efficiently without the nuisance of assemblies. Two important facts help explain why England's Parliament did not go the way of these other bodies, into political oblivion. First, because of the wars, Parliament had become an annual event, and the members had grown to know one another rather well; a corporate feeling like that which develops among the brethren of the Supreme Court had begun to emerge. Second, religious issues soon led to war at home, generating another need to recall Parliament.[11]

More than his father, Charles resolved to root out Puritans and return the Church of England to the pre-Reformation Catholic Church, minus only the pope. With his infamous archbishop William Laud and a Catholic wife, the king crusaded for religious conformity. The sacraments including Holy Communion returned. Oxford University became an orthodox institution, later burning Hobbes's *Leviathan*, the greatest work of political thought written in the English language and one of the founding texts of modern political theory, and expelling John Locke.

Charles and Laud also used the prerogative courts to stifle religious dissent. One radical Puritan polemicist, for example, was fined, disbarred, and tortured by having both his ears cut off. There was no free exercise of religion in England under Charles I.

No people reacted more violently to this religious intolerance than the Scots. By then, Scotland had an extreme Protestant heritage, thanks to the great Scottish religious reformer John Knox. When Charles and

Laud tried to force a Catholic version of the English Prayer Book on the Scots without consultation with their Parliament, riots and rebellion broke out. Fearing "the introduction of popery by the back door," the Scots took up arms and marched south into England.

Charles was forced to recall Parliament, which then poured forth a deluge of complaints about religion, money, and the king's use of prerogative courts to raise taxes illegally. In three weeks, Charles dismissed this Short Parliament, thereby causing riots and a wave of antipopery that swept through army and nation. "Things must go worse before they go better," declared John Pym, the Puritan leader of the commons.

With the Crown bankrupt, Charles had no alternative but to recall Parliament. This Long Parliament, the longest in English history, used impeachment and bills of attainder to attack the king's agents. Charles's right-hand man Thomas Wentworth was arrested, charged with high treason, impeached, and condemned to death. Following his execution, Archbishop Laud was tried and beheaded.

The Long Parliament then passed a series of radical statutes to assert control over the country. In one, it stipulated that Parliament could not be dismissed without its own consent. In another, Parliament had to assemble at least once every three years. There are similar protections of Congress in our Constitution, but the Puritans in Parliament went further. The court of Star Chamber was abolished, along with every vestige of Laud's religious policy. Another list of Charles's evil deeds, similar to our Declaration of Independence, was passed in the Grand Remonstrance. When Charles rejected it, riots in London spread, and the whole of England seemed to drift toward anarchy.

We have known a comparable anarchy only once in American history, at the dawn of the Civil War, and Abraham Lincoln, of course, met that crisis with unprecedented prerogative. Charles I was no Lincoln. Nor was Richard Nixon, and in the last days of Watergate, his advisers took advantage of his weakness by trying to wrest from him the most important prerogative a king or president possesses—control of the army and navy. Similarly, when Catholics in Ireland rebelled in 1642, Parliament took the momentous step of removing control of the military forces from the king and assuming the power to appoint all military commanders. As American law professors Douglas W. Kmiec and Stephen B. Presser note, this was "a clearly revolutionary proposition that sought, in effect, to end the King's role as commander-in-chief of the military might of the nation."[12]

This was the last straw for Charles. On January 4, 1642, he went to the House of Commons with four hundred swordsmen to arrest several prominent members. Warned of his attempt, the members had escaped. Charles entered the House of Commons—the last monarch ever to do so—and, remarking that "the birds are flown," he stormed out. A week later, he rode out of Whitehall Palace, never to return until his execution. Later that year, the king raised the royal standard and declared his Parliament in rebellion. The English Civil War, a momentous moment in the background of Anglo-American constitutionalism, had begun.

Civil War and the Trial of the King

Like our Civil War, the English Civil War was a conflict in which everyone had to choose sides and that practically no one wanted. Even after the New Model Army had defeated the king at Naseby and Charles had surrendered to the Scots, who later turned him over to Parliament, momentous constitutional questions loomed. The victors soon began fighting among themselves, and a breakdown of law and order spelled the collapse of censorship. Before then, everything written had to be approved before printing by a government censor—a practice now forbidden as a prior restraint under our Constitution. With the Civil War, the floodgates were opened and a torrent of "leaflets poured out, giving voice to the views of sections of society never heard from before—artisans, craftsmen, and ordinary working folk."

In *Federalist* No. 10, Madison would write of how enlarging the size of the republic would expand the number of factions, making it difficult for any to oppress the minority. There was certainly no shortage of factions in England in the 1640s. Numerous religious and political sects published tracts, calling for "an unprecedented overturning, questioning, and revaluing of everything which had previously been taken for granted."[13]

One particularly important group, the Levellers, attracted small farmers, craftsmen, and many followers among the rank and file of Oliver Cromwell's New Model Army. Questioning a society based on inequality and a legal system "obsessed with offenses against property,"[14] they demanded a leveling down of extremes of wealth, no property qualifications for voting, and the abolition of the House of Lords and ecclesiastical taxes.

It would be a long time before many of these Leveller ideas would be adopted in England or in America. In our country, it was not until the Jacksonian era in the 1830s that we started to end property qualifications for voting or holding office. And it was not until the twentieth century that the principle of one-person, one-vote began to be constitutionally required.

Beyond some of these specifics, however, much of the Leveller ideology does lie at the foundation of our Lockean and Jeffersonian constitutional system. "'Sovereignty lies only in the people and parliament governs only by their consent,'" the Levellers declared. Modern legal historians note the Leveller preoccupation with "the inalienable rights of the individual... [and] of the origin of government in an original compact."[15]

Oliver Cromwell and the other army officers did not agree with the Levellers that "'the poorest he that is in England' should rank with 'the greatest he.'"[16] The country would not go along with so radical an agenda, they felt, and it was the duty of the officers to persuade the rank-and-file soldiers to a more moderate settlement.

The soldiers, however, drew up their own radical constitution, the Agreement of the People, calling for abolition of the monarchy and the House of Lords and putting government in the hands of a one-house Parliament elected by universal manhood suffrage. This democracy, like American democracy 150 years later, was to be limited by a bill of rights "based on the laws of reason and nature."

It is easy to overemphasize the modern character of the Leveller ideas. Still, much in their ideology bears close comparison to American constitutionalism, as Goldwin Smith clarifies:

> Here was evolved the idea of a written constitution with paramount laws limiting the powers of government; this constitution, as all law, was to be enforceable through the courts. Here, too, appears sharply and vividly the idea that there are individual, inalienable rights possessed by all men. Mankind has been endowed by the Creator with rights such as those later more precisely defined as life, liberty, and the pursuit of happiness. . . . The Leveller and Independent ideas of democracy in seventeenth-century England united with the angry and robust voice of Sir Edward Coke to exert a powerful influence on later democratic institutional development in the United States. Some of these consequences flowed . . . through the works of such men as John Locke and the French philosophers to Thomas Jefferson and his contemporaries.[17]

It was all too early for England in 1647, however. After long debates with the soldiers at Putney Church, the officers persuaded them to modify their demands and submit them not to a nationwide referendum, but to Parliament, which soon rejected them. In the meantime, the king escaped and a second but briefer civil war erupted, ending in his recapture and complete defeat. To cleanse Parliament of royalists, Cromwell's Colonel Pride and his musketeers at the door of Westminster Hall then prevented about a hundred members from entering and imprisoned many others. When "Pride's Purge" was over, only about ninety members were left in the "Rump" of the Long Parliament, which passed an ordinance "for the trying and judging of Charles Stuart, King of England," charging him with a "wicked design totally to subvert the ancient and fundamental laws and liberties of this nation and in their place to introduce an arbitrary and tyrannical government" amounting to "treason against the people of England."[18]

Charles Stuart "laughed in the face of the court" when he was called "Tyrant and Traitor." No doubt his successor George III was not laughing when he read a similar accusation in our Declaration of Independence many years later. But Charles's reaction also invites broader legal questions with important implications for American constitutionalism as well as for international war crimes trials of modern day. Was the trial of the king legal? Could the king commit treason?

Charles certainly did not think so. Speaking on his own behalf, he asked the court "by what power I am called hither.... Remember, I am your king, your lawful king." When addressed by the lord president of the Court as an "elected king," Charles bristled. "England was never an elective kingdom, but an hereditary kingdom for near these thousand years," he replied. And Charles went on to say that he saw no Parliament—no full assembly of king, lords, and Commons. "Is this the bringing of the king to his parliament?" he asked.[19]

In a legal sense, Charles certainly was right, at least for his time. The court of Parliament would have none of his argument, however. They found Charles guilty and condemned him to death. And so, in a moment of great drama, on a scaffold erected in front of Inigo Jones's Whitehall Banqueting House, where Reubens's ceiling depicts the Stuarts as gods, Charles I was beheaded. Historian Strong tells us that the "terrible groan which went up from the watching crowd as his head fell at one stroke from his body signaled not the end of the monarchy but the inevitability of its return."[20]

From Failed Republic to Restoration and Glorious Revolution

From 1649 when Charles I died until 1660 when his son Charles II took the throne, England's constitution was a republic. It was, however, a failed republic, and this was not forgotten by the American

Founders a century and a half later. The chaotic situation in which England found itself after the king's execution has no direct parallel in our American experience. It is, however, similar to what the Federalists in 1800 feared might happen if Jefferson and his allies gained power.

After the execution of the English king, riots and religious hysteria swept the country. The Rump Parliament abolished the monarchy and the House of Lords as well as holidays like Christmas, and prescribed oaths of loyalty and the death penalty for blasphemy. Declaring your "hour has come.... You should give place to better men," Cromwell dissolved the Rump, and the army officers then chose representatives to a new Barebones Parliament, named after one of its members, Praise-God Barebone. When this assembly also failed, power was returned to the army, whose officers drew up the Instrument of Government, "England's first written constitution" and set up a Protectorate. Cromwell was to be lord protector for life, and there was to be a Council of State and a Parliament elected every three years.

Cromwell soon quarreled with this Parliament, dissolving it and dividing the country into military districts, much as the South was divided into military districts by the harsh Reconstruction Acts after the Civil War. "Sunday sports were forbidden, alehouses shut, cockfighting and horse racing banned." Cromwell ruled as a military dictator, refusing the crown like Caesar but allowing himself to be called "highness," unlike George Washington, who rejected any such title, and naming his son as his successor.

That son proved ineffectual when Cromwell died, leaving a leadership vacuum of political and social anarchy. England was sick of military rule, and just as in America before the Constitutional Convention of 1787, there was a "deep seated desire by the gentry classes for peace and social order." Conservatives united. "Royalists, businessmen, and landed Parliamentarians stood together against the army...and the leveling radicalism of the lower classes." Cromwell's heir fled, and, after an election, the new Convention Parliament declared that, "according to the ancient and fundamental laws of this kingdom the government is, and ought to be, by Kings, Lords, and Commons." The English constitution as it had developed over centuries was being restored. Promising to pardon rebels with as little blood as possible, the exiled Charles II landed at Dover and proceeded to London in a great parade "full of hope."

This Convention Parliament made a deliberate attempt to "wipe out the previous eighteen years" with a "legal fiction": "The reign of Charles II had legally begun in January, 1649, on the execution of Charles I."

Legal fictions are an important part of Anglo-American law. Even calling a corporation a person under our Fourteenth Amendment is a kind of legal fiction. Considering the constitutional development of England, however, what is significant is that the Convention Parliament in 1660 only turned the clock back to 1649, not to the days before the Civil War. The reforms of the Long Parliament were retained. The prerogative courts like Star Chamber were gone. The king might not collect taxes without Parliament's consent.

The constitutional situation, in other words, was left as vague as it had been on the eve of the king's execution. It was still "not clear which constitutional power, the executive or the legislative, had the larger say." As Thomas Hobbes wrote in 1651 in *Leviathan*, it was not clear where sovereignty was.

The importance of Hobbes's *Leviathan* for the ideas behind American constitutionalism cannot be overstated. It was, of course, from writers like Hobbes that the Founders took their assumptions about the natural equality of men, the social contract as the basis of government, and the theory of representation. There are, indeed, many passages in the Constitution and aspects of our law that are in harmony with Hobbes's teachings. There are also many others that are not. The most important of the latter is Hobbes's insistence on one absolute sovereign, without separation of powers or checks and balances. In this, of course, he also parted company with ancient philosophers like Plato, Aristotle, and Polybius, all of whom extolled the virtues of a mixed and balanced constitution. In his 1867 book *The English Constitution*, a brilliant comparison of the American presidential and English parliamentary forms of government, the English Victorian essayist Walter Bagehot shows us that this is the essence of Hobbes's positivism:

> Hobbes told us long ago... that there must be a supreme authority, a conclusive power, in every State at every point somewhere.... But there are two classes of Governments. In one, the supreme determining power is upon all points the same; in the other, that ultimate power is different upon different points, now resides in one part of the Constitution and now in another. The Americans thought they were imitating the English in making their Constitution upon the last principle—in having one ultimate authority for one sort of matter, and another for another sort. But in truth, the English constitution is the type of the opposite species; it has only one authority for all sorts of matters.

Bagehot has in mind the English constitution as it emerged after the Glorious Revolution in 1688. We will consider the constitutional consequences of that revolution shortly. For now, it is important to emphasize that, as Bagehot reminds us, Hobbes would not have liked the uncertainty and division of power characteristic of our constitutional system. "Where is your sovereign?" he would most certainly have asked us. People asked similar questions in the chaotic settlement worked out by the Convention Parliament in 1660. It was, in other words, a fragile settlement. Events were soon to prove just how fragile it could be.

The Convention Parliament was soon followed by the Cavalier Parliament, composed, like our Constitutional Convention of 1787, of "men who believed in peace and order." Under the Clarendon Code, dissenters were banned from public office. If we are inclined to the mistaken view that persecution of minorities is peculiar to American history, we would do well to notice how these laws created "a new religious underclass... which joined the Catholics, suffering persecution, harassment, and social disabilities."[21]

For his part, Charles disliked this legislation, and also resented Parliament's reluctance to vote him the money he needed to rebuild London after the plague and fire of 1665 and 1666. Like a modern imperial president, Charles turned to his inner circle of advisers, a group that came to be "called by the sinister word 'Cabal' "[22] [a word now meaning a secret political conspiracy] and began to look with eager eyes to the court of his cousin, Louis XIV of France, for inspiration.

It must be remembered that Charles had spent the better part of his exile in France. There, he saw an absolute monarch, wealthy and powerful, who, like the Roman Emperors, could claim "I am the State" (*"L'Etat, c'est moi"*). By contrast, Charles found himself ruling a state with a much impoverished crown, a plurality of faiths, and a representative assembly that made ruling more irksome.

In return for his financial assistance, Charles made a secret promise to Louis that he would become a Catholic, a promise he fulfilled only on his deathbed. Publicly, Charles issued a Declaration of Indulgence, suspending the Clarendon Code and allowing Catholics and Protestant dissenters to hold services. In reply, Parliament passed a Test Act stipulating that all public officeholders had to swear loyalty to the established Church of England and denounce Catholicism.

Our Constitution declares that "no religious Test shall ever be required as a qualification to any Office or Public Trust under the United States." In the hysteria surrounding passage of the Test Act in England in 1685, however, and Parliamentary debates over exclusion of Charles's younger Catholic brother James from succession to the throne, two rival factions—ancestors of modern-day conservative and liberal political parties—began to form. On one side, Tories emphasized devotion to royal prerogative and the Church of England. On the other, Whigs stressed toleration for Protestant dissenters, popular sovereignty, and the liberty of the subject.

When Charles got the upper hand, the leading Whig, the Earl of Shaftesbury, fled to Holland, where he later died in exile. Shaftesbury's most brilliant protégé, however, was a man who would later go on to exert a profound influence on American constitutional ideas. His name was John Locke.

We will later consider the relevance of Locke's social-contract theory to American constitutionalism. In the meantime, we need to note that, in England in 1685, Charles, like Elizabeth before him, died without an heir. He was succeeded by his brother, the haughty and openly pro-Catholic James.

This is one of those moments in constitutional history when a change in policy by one leader might have made a huge difference to the future of the legal system. We have seen others. If Pericles had not induced the Athenians to fight the war with Sparta, Athenian democracy might have endured longer and evolved in a more stable direction. If Cato had not persuaded the Romans to destroy Carthage or if Thomas Cromwell had accepted Henry VIII's plan to Romanize the common law of England, things would certainly have been different for the constitutions of republican Rome and England respectively. In our history, if Lincoln had followed the advice of many and let our erring brothers in the South depart in peace, our constitutional history would have been profoundly altered.

The same is true of James II in 1685. If he had adopted a more popular view on religion, constitutional history would have taken a decidedly different path, "for a monarchy firmly in alliance with the Church of England and the Royalist Tories…would probably have succeeded in transferring the country along the lines of the French monarchy into an absolutist state."[23]

Instead, of course, James proceeded "swiftly along the road to his own ruin."[24] Determined to restore England to Roman Catholicism, he defied the Test Act by appointing Catholics to office, then openly celebrated Mass at Whitehall and issued a new Declaration of Indulgence. When Church of England bishops called it contrary to the spirit of the constitution, James imprisoned them in the Tower and prosecuted them for seditious libel, a crime not unknown later to the American framers. When a jury acquitted the bishops, the jubilant public reaction was a sign that antagonism to the royal will was mounting. Still there was reason for patience, as the heir to the throne was to be Mary, James's Protestant daughter living in Holland. A short time of tyranny under the Catholic James could, some felt, be endured.

Then came the news that James's new Catholic wife had given birth to a son. As historian Strong puts it, for "the first time it was clear that James's reign would not be an aberration but that he could be the first of a line of Catholic kings of Great Britain." Acting swiftly, several prominent Whigs and Tories extended a formal invitation to Mary's Protestant husband, William of Orange, to come from his home in Holland to England "to aid in the restoration of English liberties."

Supported by a "Protestant wind," William landed with 15,000 troops, and everywhere in England "men hastened to serve under the banners of rebellion." Top army officers mutinied. James fled to France, encouraging anarchy in his wake by burning the writs for the new Parliament, ordering the dissolution of the army, and famously throwing the great seal of England into the river Thames. "He never saw England again."

With the English constitution once again in crisis, the House of Lords met with members of the Commons, asking the victorious William to summon a Convention, which declared that James II, "having endeavored to subvert the constitution of the kingdom by breaking the original contract between king and people,...has abdicated and the throne is thereby vacant." Although only Mary was in the bloodline of the English monarchy, her husband, William, made it clear that "he did not intend to be...merely his wife's gentleman usher." William and Mary were proclaimed joint sovereigns, the first and only time in English constitutional history when two monarchs reigned simultaneously as one.

The so-called Glorious Revolution of 1688 was completed with Parliament's passage of a Bill of Rights declaring that the king could not suspend Parliament arbitrarily or keep a standing army in peacetime without parliamentary consent, and that Catholics were to be excluded from the throne forever. From now on, no English king could sit on the throne by divine right: England was to be a constitutional monarchy. A new English constitution had been born—not ruled by a monarch alone but by the king in Parliament, as Thomas Cromwell's reforms anticipated. Rule by hereditary right "ended in England when James embarked in the darkness for France."

England's constitution, of course, went on through many more years of profound change, evolving slowly and sometimes painfully into the democratic parliamentary form of government England knows today. For the purposes of our history of the background of American constitutionalism, however, our story of English constitutional development is now essentially complete. As Corwin reminds us in *The Higher Law Background of American Constitutional Law* after the Glorious Revolution, the years of persecution were over and therefore migration to America of important classes of English dissenters virtually ended. "The colonies," he says, henceforth had to "be content for the most part with the stock of political ideas already on hand." In other words, most of the institutions and ideas of English constitutional history that were to influence the American framers were already in place by 1688 or at least by the close of the seventeenth century. It is to an examination of that influence, and the overall influence of much of the history of the ancient Athenian, Roman, and English constitutions on the formative era of American government that we now turn.

FIFTEEN

From Classical and Common Law Background to American Constitutionalism

In the previous chapter, we brought our survey of the constitutional history of England through the Glorious Revolution of 1688. A century later, our framers met in Philadelphia to design a government that owed much not only to institutions and ideas developed through English history but also to those of ancient Greece and Rome.

The result of that Philadelphia deliberation was, of course, the Constitution of the United States, a document that is regarded in America as important, sacred, and supreme. Edward S. Corwin emphasizes this American adoration of the Constitution in *The Higher Law Background of American Constitutional Law*, where he describes how other "creeds have waxed and waned, but worship of the Constitution has proceeded unabated."[1] James Randall calls attention to how both sides in the Civil War were devoted to the Constitution in his *Constitutional Problems Under Lincoln*.

Why has the Constitution been so revered in America? For one thing, it is a document of profoundly democratic origin. "We the People of the United States" created this Constitution. In Justinian's *Institutes*, whatever was pleasing to the prince had the force of law because the Roman People, by the *Lex Regia*, made over to him their whole power and authority. The American people, for their part, designated the Constitution as their supreme law, reserving to themselves the power to amend it as they should think fit.

We saw in the Introduction how the framers stressed the new democratic character of what they were doing. On one level, of course, it was not unprecedented. Democracy, understood literally as "government of the people," originated not in America in 1787 but in ancient Athens about 500 BC, as we have seen. The aristocrat Cleisthenes strengthened the democratic constitutions that Solon and Pisistratus before him had begun. Cleisthenes had a great meeting place carved out of the bare rock near the foothills of the Acropolis where an Athenian assembly composed of all free adult male citizens met regularly to discuss everything from the price of grain to declarations of war. This assembly was the ancestor not only of the Roman comitiae (assemblies) but also of the American Congress and parliaments and democratic legislatures around the world.

If their point was that democratic government was unprecedented, the American Founders were surely mistaken. On another level, there can be no denying that something was new in the democratic ratification of the American Constitution. None of the democratic states of antiquity, including Athens and Rome, had been founded by popular ratification. In the case of the Greek city-states, there was typically one lawgiver—Solon, for Athens; Lycurgus for Sparta—who inaugurated the whole enterprise. The English constitution, by contrast, like that of republican Rome, had evolved slowly, but it, too, "had never been reduced to a single composite writing and voted on by the British people or even by Parliament." As legal scholar Akhil Amar concludes, "before the American Revolution, no people had ever explicitly voted on their own written constitution." Amar is thus quite correct to say that, "with the Constitution, America could boast a breakthrough in political science. Never before had so many ordinary people been invited to deliberate and vote on the supreme law under which they and their posterity would be governed."[2]

Part of the reason for the reverence the Constitution enjoys, then, is surely its democratic origins. Then, too, however, the Constitution is regarded as sacred because of its content, because it is the "embodiment of an essential and unchanging justice." Corwin sees ideas of natural law and natural rights implicit in the due process clause and in the Ninth Amendment's reference to "other rights retained by the people." From there, he goes on to introduce his historical survey: "Whence came this idea of a 'higher law'? . . . By what agencies and as a result of what causes was it brought to America and wrought into the American system of government?"[3]

Corwin is interested primarily in the classical and English common law origins of American natural law ideas. What, however, of the influence of that background on American constitutionalism in other respects as well? Law professors Douglas Kmiec and Stephen Presser note that, although "Americans have a tendency to believe that their legal and constitutional culture is unique, . . . the simple fact is that our governing philosophy, our Constitution, and our laws reflect the experience of thousands of years of world civilization." It has been to a large extent the burden of this book to emphasize and it will be the burden of this chapter to recapitulate "how much of what happens in American politics and law today is but a continuation of a conversation among humankind stretching back thousands of years."[4]

Like Corwin, Kmiec and Presser deny that the Constitution framers intended to displace the fundamental principles of the Declaration of Independence. Instead, they cite Madison's invocation of the Declaration as the "first of the 'best guides' to the distinctive principles" of our government.[5] The famous Preamble to the Declaration is based on two fundamental ideas that reflect the long classical and English tradition from which they are derived:

> We hold these truths to be self-evident, that all men are created equal, that they are endowed by their Creator with certain unalienable Rights, that among these are Life, Liberty, and the pursuit of Happiness; That to secure these rights, Governments are instituted among Men, deriving their just powers from the consent of the governed. That whenever any Form of Government becomes destructive of those ends, it is the Right of the People to alter or to abolish it.[6]

In speaking here of self-evident truths and elsewhere of "the laws of Nature and of Nature's God," Jefferson is clearly invoking the natural law tradition, the outline of which we have seen and that Corwin in his essay is at pains to survey. In speaking of the "consent of the governed" and the "Right of the People," Jefferson is just as obviously invoking a tradition of popular sovereignty, democracy, and representation—a tradition with an equally long history and background, as we have noted.

In considering the classical origins of Jefferson's conception of natural law, Corwin begins his account, as we began this book, with the ancient Greeks. He mentions Demosthenes's observation that "every law is a discovery," and Antigone's "appeal against Creon's edict to the 'unwritten and steadfast customs of the gods'" in Sophocles's play. He also cites Aristotle's treatment of natural justice in *The Ethics* as well as his observation, in *The Rhetoric*, that a lawyer who has no case at law will tend to "'appeal to the law of nature.'"[7]

We saw in our historical survey of Athenian constitutional history that in archaic times only the nobles had the power to discover law. Later, as we noted, first Draco and then Solon and Cleisthenes worked those "discovered" principles into a written code that all could learn. Noting American parallels to these ideas, Corwin cites President Calvin Coolidge's observation that men "'do not make laws. They do but discover them.'"[8] He might also have cited the many references to natural law and natural justice in the cases of the United States Supreme Court (some of which we reviewed in the chapters on the Greek and Roman constitutions).

Like natural justice, popular sovereignty also has its roots in the ancient Greek world in general and in Athens in particular. As we saw, the Greeks set the West on its humanist path, and, in the ancient Greek tradition, our Constitution begins not with an invocation of the gods as do the ancient codes of Hammurabi and Lipit-Ishtar, but rather with the simple and elegant phrase "We the People." Socrates explained to Crito that he could not escape prison because doing so would violate the "agreement" between the citizen and the laws. Similarly, our Constitution is based on a social compact between rulers and ruled.

In recalling ancient Greek origins of the popular sovereignty ideas implicit in the Declaration, however, we must acknowledge that the American framers did not take ancient Greek democracy and make it ours. First, the ancient Greeks never had full democracy, if by that term we mean participation by all members of society. More important, however, the American framers rejected direct democracy. The new president was to be elected, not directly by the people, but by an Electoral College, the Senate by the state legislatures, and the Supreme Court appointed for life by the president.

James Madison is particularly careful to emphasize that the new form of government is a republic and not a democracy in *Federalist* No. 10, and both he and Hamilton stress the republican over the democratic features of the new system throughout *The Federalist Papers*. But then the American framers were not the first to see in the ancient Greek world a lesson of the dangers rather than the virtues of democracy. Plato and Aristotle certainly saw that, and with justification. The history of ancient Athens especially after Pericles was a history of demagoguery, anarchy, and mob democracy run rampant. It was this sort of anarchy that the American framers saw in democracy and wanted to avoid.

Polybius, the great pupil of Aristotle and author of the *History of Rome*, recognized that the way to avoid that precipitous decline into mob rule was through a carefully balanced mixed constitution. Not all philosophers since the ancients have admired such a system. Hobbes, as we saw, did not. Nor did Rousseau, who compares advocates of the mixed constitution to Japanese magicians in his revolutionary *Contract Social*, published a generation before our country's founding:

> Japanese sleight of hand artists are said to dismember a child before the eyes of spectators, then, throwing all the parts in the air one after the other, they make the child fall back down alive

and all in one piece. These conjuring acts of our political theorists are more or less like these performances. After having taken
apart the social body by means of a sleight of hand worthy of a
carnival, they put the pieces back to together, who knows how.[9]

Other early modern philosophers, such as John Locke, clearly embraced
the idea of the mixed constitution, however, and the American framers were directly influenced by these writers as well as by the ancient
Greek background whom Polybius, in his *Histories*, had in mind.

It was not Athenian democracy that so attracted the framers; it
was their emphasis on the rule of law. We saw how central this idea
was for the Greeks—how it helped them distinguish themselves, as
Hellenes, from the Barbarians around them. We also emphasized
how central the rule of law is to us in America. As Tom Paine put it
in *Common Sense* in the year of our Declaration of Independence, "in
America, the law is king."[10]

With an eye to the importance of the rule of law, Corwin turns
from the Greeks to the Romans, and there he emphasizes (as in the
earlier chapter on Rome), the writings of Cicero. Central to that great
jurist's conception, as Corwin notes, is the point that written human
laws and justice are not necessarily the same and that human laws
can be evaluated by how they measure up against justice or natural
law: "Not all things are necessarily just which are established by the
civil laws and institutions of nations, [nor is] justice identical with
obedience to the written laws.... If it were possible to constitute right
simply by the commands of the people,... then all that would be necessary in order to make robbery, adultery, or the falsification of wills
right and just would be a vote of the multitude."[11]

Cicero also asserts that natural law requires no higher interpretation than that of the individual. In our formative era, the Jefferso-
nians wanted juries to exercise judicial review, a power traceable, in
part, to this Ciceronian vision of a higher law. Although Chief Justice
Marshall reserved this power for courts, ruling in *Marbury v. Madison* that it is "primarily the province and duty of the judicial depart-

ment to say what the law is," even today, all government officials in America engage in constitutional interpretation. Moreover, Cicero's notion of the individual character of legal reasoning was reinforced for the framers by the legacy of the Reformation. In Robert Bolt's play *A Man for All Seasons* about the martyrdom of Sir Thomas More, Henry VIII asks, "Does a man need a Pope to tell him he has sinned?" In legal terms, one might ask, "Does a man need a Judge to tell him when something violates the people's fundamental law?"

Corwin also reminds us of the vital importance of our long survey of ancient Rome's constitutional development when he says that Cicero wrote at a particularly crucial time in Rome's history. His ideas thus "brought the Stoic conception of a universal law into contact with Roman law at the moment when the administrators of the latter were becoming aware of the problem of adapting a rigid and antique code... [to] an empire which already overshadowed the Mediterranean world."[12] We, too, face the challenge of adapting a two-hundred-year-old constitution to the demands of leadership in an increasingly complex world.

The emphasis on Cicero in Corwin's essay reminds us of the Roman origins of our natural law tradition. The idea of the sovereignty of the people is also, in part, Roman in origin, however, as we have seen. Like the kings of archaic Greece, the Roman kings before the Republic had their decrees ratified by the rank-and-file soldiers. In the Republic, assemblies or comitiae continued to bring together the citizens for direct participation in government. The difference from us is, of course, that when they spoke of the rule of the people, the ancient Romans, like the Greeks, meant direct rule. They would not have understood our representative and republican form of government. That is why Aristotle says a city-state should be small enough that everyone in the city could know one another by name.

The word *Republic* is derived, of course, from the Roman *res publica* (public thing). In more modern times, it is the English theorist Hobbes, as we saw, who gives us the first well-developed theory of representative government. Before Hobbes, however, stretches the long historical development of English representative institutions, including both the jury and Parliament, the details of which we considered earlier at some length. Reviewing that history, Corwin notes John of Salisbury, "the first systematic writer on politics in the Middle Ages," and his distinction between a tyrant "who oppresses the people by rule based upon force" and a "prince" or "one who rules in accordance with the laws."

Representative institutions were not the only contributions that the long history of English constitutionalism made to American law, however. The English common law, as it developed down to Tudor and Stuart times, is clearly the background against which the American Constitution must be understood.

When he was a young, unemployed lawyer of twenty-eight on the eve of the American Revolution, John Adams wrote that "the unalienable, indefeasible rights of man . . . were never so skillfully and successfully consulted as in that most excellent monument of human reason, the common law of England."[13] Corwin says American statesmen of Adams's generation ascribed a "transcendental quality" to the common law and "above all to its vast antiquity." When the Revolution did come, the Founding Fathers saw themselves fighting to preserve rights that had been worked out by the English courts in the development of the common law.

Today there is no more telling statement of American constitutionalism than to say that ours is a common law nation. But the common law for us is not what it originally meant for the framers. Today, *common law* means "judge-made law"—law made by judges, through cases, and extended by precedent. At the time of our constitutional framing, the term meant a preexisting body of rules that judges did not create but discovered. James Stoner explains this original meaning in *Common Law Liberty*, making reference to institutions and historical trends that we examined:

Common law was, in the first place, the immemorial customary law of England, enforced in the Court of Common Pleas and the

King's Bench.... The written evidence of common law was to be found in the records of cases previously decided. To learn the law meant to learn those precedents and the rules of law they established.... In deciding cases, it was the judge's duty to discover, not invent, what law governed the case at hand. If a case seemed genuinely novel, the judge was to proceed by analogy to the appropriate precedent.[14]

American law today is also "found in the records of cases previously decided." American law students still "learn those precedents and the rules of law they established." American judges today still claim "to discover, not invent" the law and also "proceed by analogy to the appropriate precedent."

Stoner goes on to note that the "larger principles of the English constitution clearly bore the stamp of common-law thinking." So, too, did the writings of the American framers, who were not reluctant to claim the English common law as their rightful inheritance. The First Continental Congress proclaimed that the "respective colonies are entitled to the common law of England." The Declaration of Independence gives a long list of rights at common law that the king had violated. As the colonies became states and wrote their state constitutions, they "received" part of the common law of England, as modified to adapt to the more egalitarian and democratic spirit of the New World.

In the 1787 Constitution, there are a number of terms that can only be understood with reference to English common law–like habeas corpus and ex post facto and phrases such as "during good behavior." Article III extends the judicial power to cases "in Law and Equity"—a direct reference to the English tradition of common law courts and courts of equity. This same Article also guarantees trial by jury, one of the hallmarks of the English common law tradition. The framers clearly saw the federal judiciary in common law terms. In *Federalist* No. 78, Hamilton assumes that the federal judges will be "bound down by strict rules and precedents" and will have to commit themselves to "long and laborious study" of the "records of precedents." The Bill of Rights also enshrines many common law privileges. In the Seventh Amendment, the right of trial by jury is preserved in suits at common law.

In sum, it is impossible to understand the American Constitution without understanding the English common law tradition that pre-dated it. When reviewing common law history from its pre-Norman origins to the Tudor and Stuart eras, we focused on English common law being based on custom, in sharp contrast with the European con-tinent where, as Corwin explains, "custom remained till the French Revolution purely local." This is because, on the continent, feudalism divided whereas in England, Norman feudalism united the realm as it never had been before. Then, too, as Corwin notes, the "right reason to which the maxims of higher law on the Continent were addressed was always the right reason invoked by Cicero, it was the right reason of all men. The right reason which lies at the basis of the common law, on the other hand, was from the beginning judicial right reason."[15] This is why Coke told King James I, as we said, that judicial reason-ing requires expertise and long study and is not the same as natural reason. Law in our English common law tradition has a reasoning of its own.

With an eye to the development of that reasoning, the great American twentieth-century legal scholar Roscoe Pound emphasized that the "events of legal history are in truth acts of definite men," and Corwin agrees that "the history of the common law is far from being a mere anonymous tradition."[16] We have already seen many of the great names in that tradition, including monarchs such as Henry VIII and his chancellor Thomas Cromwell. Then, too, there are the great judicial commentators on the common law. Corwin mentions Brac-ton and the tradition of the rule of law.

Also stressing the rule of law, John Orth notes the phrase "due process" was not "invented by American constitution writers; it was picked up by them from the rich tradition of English constitution-alism in which they were formed."[17] Orth describes how the due process clause can be traced back to Magna Carta, which the framers regarded as the fountainhead of English liberties. In addition to Magna Carta and Coke, Corwin emphasizes the writings of Sir John Fortescue, chief justice under Henry VI (reigned 1422–1461), who wrote that it was "not customary for the kings of England to sit in court or pronounce judgment themselves."[18] When Coke reminded James I of that fact, he precipitated, as we saw, one of the great battles over the common law as a limit on royal power. In Bracton's day, there had been no such limit; the only redress against tyranny was divine retribution. It was Coke and the English Civil War that finally established how the common law and the constitution can impose effective limits on royal power.

Corwin correctly points out the link between what Coke says in Dr. Bonham's Case about "common right and reason" and the long natural law tradition going back to Cicero and the Romans then ahead to Locke and Jefferson's "self-evident principles." Coke specified what many of those "self-evident principles" are, and his axioms "early found their way into American judicial decisions." Corwin mentions the principle that a "statute should have prospective, not retroactive, effect," linking it to our constitutional ban on ex post facto laws. Another Coke maxim that "no one should be twice punished for the same offense" became embodied in our Fifth Amendment as the double jeopardy clause. Then, too, Corwin says, Coke stresses that "every man's home is his castle," a principle that lies at the root of our Fourth Amendment prohibition on unreasonable searches.

If Coke's maxim about the common law in Dr. Bonham's Case foreshadows judicial review, there must be a link between Coke's ideas and the arguments of Chief Justice Marshall, whose famous opinion in *Marbury v. Madison* is, again, the genesis of judicial review in America. In *Marbury*, Marshall assumes that it is the judiciary that decides constitutional questions. But Corwin rightly warns us to be wary of concluding that Coke also "regarded the ordinary courts of law as the final authoritative interpreters." Here, Coke, true to the ambiguities of his era, temporized where Marshall, writing 150 years later, did not. Marshall was uncategorical: "It is emphatically the province and duty of the judicial department to say what the law is." Coke, however, "regarded the ordinary courts as peculiarly qualified to interpret and apply the law of reason, [but] he also...recognized the superior claims of the High Court of Parliament as a law declaring body." For Coke, the "power and jurisdiction of Parliament...is so transcendent and absolute as it cannot be confined, within any bounds." And yet, Coke also says that Magna Carta is above any ordinary statute. It is, as he puts it, "such a fellow that he will have no 'Sovereign.'"[19]

Coke's ambiguity on sovereignty must, of course, be understood in the context of his times. There was no consensus that the king or Parliament was sovereign. To appreciate how this ambivalence changed, in America, into the certitude of Marshall's statement about the judicial role, we have to consider intellectual developments in England in the century after Coke—a century that generated many constitutional ideas, which "were carried across the Atlantic to exert their influence on American constitutions."[20]

Corwin tells us that natural law ideas dominated English thinking from the Glorious Revolution into the eighteenth century and that the continued prestige of this doctrine was due primarily to the work of Hugo Grotius and Sir Isaac Newton. Grotius, writing on the continent, revived the Ciceronian Roman Law concept of natural law, insisting that even God Himself could not make two plus two equal other than four. As for Newton, his "demonstration that the force which brings the apple to the ground is the same force that holds the planets in their orbits stirred his contemporaries with the picture of a universe which is pervaded with the same reason...accessible in all its parts to exploration by man." From Newton, "systems were elaborated which purported to deduce with Euclidian precision the whole duty of man, both moral and legal, from a few agreed premises."

It is certainly not a long way from that Newtonian universe to the "self-evident truths" of Jefferson's Declaration, but Corwin is correct to note that, beyond Newton, the "conveyance of natural law ideas into

American constitutional theory was the work pre-eminently, though not exclusively, of John Locke's Second Treatise of Government, which appeared in 1690 as an apology for the Glorious Revolution."

In *Political Representation in England: The Origins of the American Republic*, J. R. Pole of Cambridge says that "scholars have discovered the spirit of Locke brooding...in the woods of America." In reality, there is, he insists, "very little evidence" that "Locke exerted any effective influence on the political thought of the colonists until Thomas Jefferson came to draft the Declaration of Independence."[21]

Pole correctly reminds us that social contract ideas were deeply rooted in America long before Locke. The Mayflower Compact, the first governing document of Plymouth Colony, proves, as Corwin says, that "more than two generations before Locke's Second Treatise, a social compact was conceived as supplying the second permanent government within what is now the United States."[22] Moreover, Coke's ideas, not Locke's, influenced the early development of law in colonial America. The influence of his doctrines helps explain, for example, the "efforts of colonial legislatures to secure for their constituencies the benefits of Magna Carta" as well as the decisions of courts to hold local taxes contrary to fundamental law, an argument revived in the following century by James Otis in the Writs of Assistance Case.

"If the seventeenth century was Coke's" in America, however, "the early half of the eighteenth was Locke's, especially in New England." Through their "sermons and controversial pamphlets, the New England clergy taught their flocks political theory, and...after the Bible, Locke was the principal authority."

Locke teaches in the *Second Treatise* that "the first and fundamental positive law of all commonwealths is the establishing of the legislative power."[23] The American framers would follow this precept a century later when they put the legislative power in Article I of the Constitution. Although this authority is, for Locke, "sacred and unalterable in the hands where the community have once placed it," it is no absolute power "to rule by extemporary, arbitrary decrees, but is bound to dispense justice...by promulgated standing laws." In our

Constitution, too, the legislative power is not absolute. It is confined by Article I, Section 9, which lists the powers denied to Congress, as well as by the Bill of Rights, which enumerates limits on Congress's powers.

Other important Lockean contributions to American constitutional thought include his famous defense of the natural right of property and labor theory of value, which became "the cornerstone of the doctrine of laissez-faire" as well as an anticipation of Marx's later use of the same theory for opposite ends. Then, too, there is Locke's chapter on prerogative, where he says that "several things should be left to the discretion of him that has the executive power." This chapter inspired Alexander Hamilton to write in *The Federalist Papers* that implied government powers are necessary because "it is impossible to foresee and define the extent and variety of national exigencies or of the means which may be necessary to satisfy them." It also lies behind Marshall's defense of implied power in *McCulloch v. Maryland* as well as Lincoln's defense of his prerogative powers in the Civil War and the justifications of emergency power of every wartime president from Wilson to today.

Corwin tells us that Locke took the doctrine of natural law and, influenced by the English common law tradition as elaborated by Coke and by the commonwealth tradition as articulated by the Levellers, developed it into a doctrine of natural rights. The ultimate right, Locke says, is the right of the people to rebel against a tyrant who has broken the social contract, although only after what Jefferson and Locke both called a "long train of abuses." This focus on natural rights and the ultimate right to rebel was "just what the doctor ordered" in the 1760s and 1770s in America, as the attention of the colonists began to turn to what they increasingly saw as the oppression of the mother country. As Corwin reminds us, just about this same time, "the first generation of the American bar was coming to maturity—students of Coke, and equipped to bring his doctrines to the support of Locke should the need arise."

Corwin says that the "opening gun in the controversy leading to the Revolution was Otis's argument in 1761 in the Writs of Assistance Case." Echoing Coke's dictum, Otis said that an "act against the Constitution is void; an Act against natural Equity is void." "Then and there," John Adams later wrote, "the child Independence is born." Corwin adds "that then and there American constitutional law is born, for Otis's contention goes far beyond Coke's; an ordinary court may traverse the specifically enacted will of Parliament, and its condemnation is final."[24]

Adams used a similar argument against the Stamp Act. Both he and Otis, as well as other leading revolutionary theorists, were well acquainted with the ancient and English constitutions, and were as influenced by past lessons of Greek, Roman, and Stuart despotism as they were by theories of "Rights antecedent to all earthly government."

"From the destructive phase of the Revolution," Corwin says, "we turn to its constructive phase"—what historian Bernard Bailyn calls the single most prolific period of constitution making in history. As former colonies became states, they wrote state constitutions enlarging the legislative power and reducing the executive power they associated with royal tyranny. Underlying these constitutions, Corwin adds, was the assumption that "the rights of the individual have nothing to fear from majority rule exercised through legislative assemblies chosen for brief terms by a restricted, though on the whole democratic electorate."

The renewed faith in legislative supremacy in the new states during the 1770s can also be traced to the long history of popular sovereignty—from the direct democracy of the ancient Athenians and republican Romans to the witan of Saxon England and the rise of the English Parliament. The most direct source of the idea of absolute legislative supremacy in America, however, was Blackstone's *Commentaries*, of which, before the Revolution, nearly 2,500 copies had been sold on this side of the Atlantic.

First published at Oxford between 1765 and 1769, the *Commentaries* are a four-volume summary of the common law. It has been said that the appeal of this treatise in the formative era of American law may have been due, in part, to its readable style and its usefulness "as a ready reference for many lawyers and jurists." John Marshall's father was a subscriber to the first Philadelphia printing of the *Commentaries* in 1771, and Marshall's great adversary Thomas Jefferson called Blackstone's treatise "the most elegant and best digested" of any English work on law, "rightfully taking [its] place by the side of the Justinian *Institutes*." Although Jefferson as a law student had been critical of some passages in Blackstone and later warned that the popularity of his book "encouraged a too-slavish reliance on English precedent," he did welcome the first American annotated editions of the *Commentaries*, which appeared while Jefferson was president in 1804.[25]

Blackstone influenced American law long beyond Marshall and Jefferson. Lincoln is said to have learned law by reading Blackstone. In the late nineteenth century, jurists such as Thomas Cooley published new American editions of the work and "converted the Blackstonian conservatism into the laissez-faire principles that dominated American constitutional law until the 1930s."

Blackstone has been credited with coining the phrase "pursuit of happiness," which later, of course, found its way into Jefferson's Declaration of Independence. Like Coke and Locke and so many others before him, Blackstone does talk about natural law, but he equates it with the will of God. Unlike some of his Ciceronian predecessors, Blackstone's focus is on the state of law of his own day—"never to any more exalted standard" of higher law.

In the time of Henry VIII, Thomas Cromwell helped establish the principle that only the king in Parliament is sovereign. It took more than a century of reformation, civil war, and the Glorious Revolution for England finally to accept that doctrine. Hobbes had understood it in 1650, writing in *Leviathan* that there must be an absolute sovereign somewhere. Blackstone took that same position and, applying the lessons of a century more of history, did not hesitate to assign to Parliament that exalted role. There "is and must be in all [states] ... a supreme, irresistible, absolute, uncontrolled authority," Blackstone says, and "the law-making power in Great Britain is Parliament, in which, therefore, sovereignty resides." Blackstone emphatically rejects judicial review. He says that "if the parliament will positively enact [an unreasonable law], there is no power in the ordinary forms of the constitution that is vested with authority to control it." Judges, he goes on, are not "at liberty to reject" acts of Parliament, for that "were to set the judicial power above that of the legislative which would be subversive of all governments."[26]

Such a doctrine may seem the antithesis of American constitutionalism, with our tradition of judicial review. Yet Jefferson said much the same thing, and Lincoln said in his First Inaugural that "if the policy of the government, upon vital questions, affecting the whole people, is to be irrevocably fixed by... the Supreme Court,... the people will have ceased to be their own rulers, having... practically resigned their government into the hands of that eminent tribunal."

America has a long history of popular sovereignty, with roots not only in Blackstone but also in ancient democracy and the English representative tradition. It can be seen most pointedly in the Jacksonian era, as well as in FDR's battle against the Nine Old Men of the Supreme Court in the 1930s. To this day, it reappears every time a Supreme Court justice, urging judicial restraint, says that the Court should accept the popular will unless it transgresses a specific prohibition in the Constitution. Justice Antonin Scalia embraces that Blackstonian vision on the Court today: "It just seems to me incompatible with democratic theory [to say] that it's good and right for the state to do something that the majority of the people do not want done.... If the people, for example, want abortion, the state should permit abortions in a democracy. If the people do not want it, the state should be able to prohibit it as well."[27]

If popular sovereignty has remained such a vital tradition in American law, why didn't it extinguish the natural law/natural-rights tradition in the way that it did in England? Just as we asked why English law never became Romanized, so, too, we must ask why

American law never became thoroughly Anglicized and why we never wholly accepted the English doctrine, worked out through centuries of war and epitomized in Blackstone, that the legislature "can do anything except make a man a woman or a woman a man."

The answer Corwin gives to this question is that, unlike the British, we had, from the start, a written Constitution, and our judges asserted, from the start, a power of judicial review, both of which acted as limits on popular sovereignty. The English common law tradition was, of course, that of a nation without a written Constitution. In this respect, the act of the American Founding Fathers in Philadelphia in 1787 was, to be sure, something quite new.

Conclusion

Unlike the constitutions of the ancient Romans and the English, which evolved over centuries and were never reduced to a single document, the American Constitution was written down in one single famous act. This is, according to McIlwain, what Thomas Paine meant when he wrote that "there is no Constitution in England" and that "a Government without a Constitution is power without right." McIlwain contrasts Paine's conception of a Constitution with that of English law of that age. He quotes Henry St. John, Viscount Bolingbroke, who wrote in 1733 that by constitution we mean "that assemblage of laws, institutions, and customs, derived from fixed principles of reason, directed to certain fixed objects of public good, that compose the general system, according to which the community hath agreed to be governed."[1]

And yet, McIlwain says, Paine's is surely the more modern conception of constitution: "Whatever we may think of it theoretically, Paine's notion that the only true constitution is one consciously constructed, and that a nation's government is only the creature of this constitution, conforms probably more closely than any other to the actual development of the world since the opening of the nineteenth century."[2]

One after another, nations around the world have adopted written constitutions. Few, however, have also followed America in giving courts judicial review. Corwin is thus correct to say that part of the reason America never lost the natural law tradition is our unique written Constitution and our doctrine of judicial review.

The deeper explanation for American constitutional exceptionalism, however, is that America is the heir of two opposite traditions—the tradition of popular sovereignty, with its roots in ancient democracy and the English parliamentary system, theorized by Hobbes and Blackstone, on the one hand, and the natural law tradition echoing back to Cicero and the Romans as well as Bracton, Coke, and Locke, on the other. In a larger sense, American constitutionalism also combines two other vital principles from its ancient and English antecedents. One is the mixed regime, endorsed by the ancient Greeks, put into practice by republican Rome and England with its evolving constitution of king, lords, and Commons, and embraced in modern times by political philosophers from Locke to Madison. The other is representation—a principle explicitly rejected by the ancients but that grew in England from the common law jury of Henry II, the Model Parliament of Edward I, the Reformation Parliament of Thomas Cromwell, the Long Parliament of the English Civil War, and beyond to the Restoration and Glorious Revolution.

American constitutionalism is a mix of all of these traditions. And there is one other relevant mix as well—of idealism and realism. From the ancient Greeks, America inherited a preoccupation with civic virtue as a restraint on tyranny, a theme that also dominated the writings of leading English Whig theorists from James Harrington, whose *Commonwealth of Oceana* was an application of Aristotle to English society; to Algernon Sydney and Viscount Bolingbroke. But there has been a competing tradition in America—a tradition of practical realism that we owe as much to the ancient Romans as to Machiavelli. As modern political philosopher Joseph Cropsey has put it, in America the "'hard' modernity of Machiavelli" and of Rome has merged with the "soft modernity of Hobbes and Locke."

In our tradition of democratic popular sovereignty and natural rights, our mixed constitution and representative institutions, our idealism and realism, we stand today as heirs of the great constitutional legacies of the ancient Greeks and Romans and the English. Learning the history of the development of the constitutions of those three great civilizations can thus add immeasurably to our own appreciation of our rich heritage and of the Western constitutional tradition, the torch of which we proudly bear.

NOTES

INTRODUCTION

1. 487 U.S. 654 (1988).
2. 343 U.S. 579 (1952).
3. Akhil Reed Amar, *America's Constitution: A Biography* (New York: Random House), 5.
4. Amar, 7.
5. Ibid.
6. Richard Randall, *American Constitutional Development*, vol. 1 (New York: Addison Wesley Longman, 2002), 92.
7. Charles Howard McIlwain, *Constitutionalism: Ancient and Modern*, rev. ed. (Ithaca, NY / London: Cornell University Press, 1947), 9.
8. Ibid., 1.

CHAPTER I: ANCIENT GREECE AND AMERICAN CONSTITUTIONALISM

1. *McCulloch v. Maryland*, 17 U.S. 316 (1819).
2. Quoted in C. E. Robinson, *Zito Hellas: A Short History of Ancient Greece* (London: Chapman and Hall, 1946), 13.
3. Ibid., 25.
4. Ibid., 49.
5. *Originalism: A Quarter Century of Debate*, ed. S. Calabresi (Washington, DC: Regnery, 2007), 3.
6. Edwin Meese, Speech Before the American Bar Association, July 9, 1985, in *Originalism*, 47.
7. H. N. Couch, *Classical Civilization: Greece*, 2nd ed. (Upper Saddle River, NJ: Prentice Hall).

8. Henry Paolucci, *A Brief History of Political Thought and Statecraft*, published for the Bagehot Council by Griffon House, 46.
9. H. D. F. Kitto, *The Greeks* (London: Penguin Books, 1957), 64–65.
10. Ibid.
11. Quoted in Steinberger, *Readings in Classical Political Thought*, 40–41.
12. Aristotle, *Politics*, 1:2.
13. Robert Morkot, foreword to *Penguin Historical Atlas of Classical Greece* (London: Penguin Books, 1996).

CHAPTER 2: THE EVOLUTION OF ATHENIAN DEMOCRACY: MODEL AND CONTRAST FOR AMERICAN DEMOCRATIC DEVELOPMENT

1. Robinson, 26.
2. His address is one of the most biting antiwar speeches in literature, rivaled only in modern times by passages in Shakespeare's *Henry V*.
3. Couch, 206.
4. Stringfellow Barr, *The Will of Zeus* (Philadelphia: J. B. Lippincott, 1961), ch. 4.
5. Steinberger, *Political Thought*.
6. See Douglas MacDowell, *The Law in Classical Athens* (Ithaca, NY: Cornell University Press, 1978).
7. See C. E. Robinson, *Zito Hellas*.
8. Thucydides, *History of the Peloponnesian War*, translated with an introduction by Rex Warner (Middlesex, England: Penguin Classics, 1954), 22.

CHAPTER 3: THE EMPIRE OF REASON: SOCRATES, PLATO, AND ARISTOTLE

1. Peter Steinberger, *Readings in Classical Political Thought*, 19.
2. Ibid.
3. *Palko v. Connecticut*, 302 U.S. 319 (1937) and *Adamson v. California*, 332 U.S. 46 (1947). See generally *Leading Constitutional Cases on Criminal Justice*, ed. Lloyd Weinreb (New York: Foundation Press, 2010), 3–24.
4. Model Penal Code, Sec. 2.01(1) and Commentary.
5. Plato, *Apology*, 26a, in Steinberger, *Readings in Classical Political Thought*, 151–2.
6. Model Penal Code, Section 2.01(2)(d).
7. *Bratty v. Attorney General* [1963], excerpted in Sanford H. Kadish and Stephen J. Schulhofer, *Criminal Law and Its Processes*, 7th ed. (Gaithersburg, NY: Aspen Law and Business, 2001), 177.
8. Wayne R. Lafave and Austin W. Scott, Jr., *Criminal Law*, 2nd ed. (St. Paul, MN: West, 1986), 643.

CHAPTER 4: ROME, AMERICA, AND THE IMPORTANCE OF ROMAN LAW

1. David Dudley, *The Civilization of Rome* (New York: NAL, 1960), 10.
2. Cullen Murphy, *Are We Rome?* (New York: Houghton Mifflin, 2007), 4–5.
3. Ibid., 35–39.
4. Ibid., 6–17.
5. Ibid., 14–15
6. Ibid., 6–17
7. Dudley, 10.
8. Hans Julius Wolff, *Roman Law: An Historical Introduction* (Norman: University of Oklahoma Press, 1951), 3.
9. Henry Paolucci, *Lectures on Roman History* (Smyrna, DE: Griffon House, 2004), 7.
10. Barry Nicholas, *An Introduction to Roman Law,* 1.
11. Wolff, 3–4.
12. Wolff, 4.
13. Nicholas, 2.
14. Paolucci, *Lectures on Roman History,* 9.
15. Douglas Kmiec and Stephen Presser, *The History, Philosophy, and Structure of the American Constitution* (Cincinnati: Anderson Publishing, 1998), 135.
16. Quoted in Kmiec and Presser, Cicero, *De Legibus,* bks. 1 and 2, trans. Clinton Keyes, 1928).
17. Cicero, *De Re Publica,* bk. 3, 211.
18. *Calder v. Bull,* 3 U.S. (3 Dall.) 386 (1798).
19. William J. Brennan, "Speech to the Text and Teaching Symposium," Georgetown University, 1985, in *Originalism: A Quarter Century of Debate,* ed. S. Calabresi.
20. James Madison, *Federalist* No. 51.

CHAPTER 5: ROMAN LAW AND AMERICAN LAW: COMPARISONS AND CONTRASTS

1. James Burnham, *An Introduction to the Law and Legal System of the United States,* 3d ed. (St. Paul, MN: West Group/A Thomason, 2000), 246.
2. Cases concerning inheritance were the most common in ancient Rome, and cases involving personal injury—what we would call the law of torts—seem to have been relatively rare. See Andrew Borkowski, *Textbook on Roman Law,* 2nd ed. (Oxford: Oxford University Press, 1997), 66.
3. Borkowski, 63–64.
4. See Abraham Ordover, *Alternatives to Litigation,* cited in Burnham, 246n113.
5. See Burnham, 119.
6. Ibid., 67.
7. Wolff, 77–78.

8.   This omits the important distinction in ancient Rome between free men and *freedmen*, those who had been freed from slavery. Like the newly freed slaves of post–Civil War America, freedmen in Rome were subject to a number of legal disabilities. See Borkowski, 103.

9.   "There are many points in our law in which the condition of females is inferior to that of males" (*Digest* 1.5.9). Is our law always so candid?

10. Even some *sui iuris* persons needed a guardian in Rome—young children, women, minors, spendthrifts, and the insane. Guardianship is, of course, also very important in our law as well.

11. Later in Christianized Rome, the killing of newborn infants was declared parricide.

12. Adoption Act, 1926. Referenced in Burnham, 135.

CHAPTER 6: ROMAN LAW FROM THE MONARCHY TO THE REPUBLIC

1.   Nicholas, 3.

2.   Dudley, 24.

3.   Guglielmo Ferrero and Corrado Barbagallo, *A Short History of Rome: The Monarchy and Republic* (New York: Capricorn Books, 1964), 21–23.

4.   Alexander Hamilton, *Federalist* No. 70.

5.   Polybius, *Histories*, bk. 6.

6.   Cowell says that it "seems highly probable that the battle of Cannae (216 BC), a defeat that very nearly brought the state to ruin, was lost mainly because of this divided command" (170).

7.   Ibid.

8.   Ibid.

9.   Wolff, 61.

CHAPTER 7: THE REPUBLIC IN DECLINE AND THE EMPIRE

1.   Paolucci, *Lectures on Roman History*, 9.

2.   Polybius, *History*, 1:3:4.

3.   Paolucci, *Lectures on Roman History*, 53

4.   Ibid., 54.

5.   Ibid., 66–67.

6.   Ibid., 71.

7.   Ibid.,100.

8.   Ibid., 107.

CHAPTER 8: THE IMPORTANCE AND ORIGINS OF THE ENGLISH CONSTITUTION

1. *See* Walter Bagehot, *The English Constitution.* (Ithaca, NY: Cornell University Press, 1961). *See also* Karl Loewenstein, *British Cabinet Government* (New York: Oxford University Press, 1967).
2. Thomas Hobbes, *Leviathan,* 1:16, 2:17.
3. F. W. Maitland, *The Constitutional History of England* (Cambridge: Cambridge University Press, 1963), 70–74.
4. Maitland, 22–23.
5. James Stoner, *Common Law Liberty* (Lawrence: University Press of Kansas, 2003), 1–5.
6. Norman Cantor, *Imagining the Law: Common Law and the Foundations of the American Legal System* (New York: HarperCollins, 1997), xii.
7. J. H. Baker, *An Introduction to English Legal History,* 2nd ed. (Butterworths, 1979), 2.
8. Cantor, 35.
9. See J. B. Bury, *History of the Later Roman Empire,* who argues that the loss of Britain in 407 led directly to the losses of Spain and parts of Africa. Cited by Frederick Pollock and F. W. Maitland, *The History of English Law Before the Time of Edward I* (Union, NJ: The Lawbook Exchange, 1996), 5n3
10. Maitland, 1.
11. Cantor, 27.
12. Maitland, 1.
13. Pollock and Maitland, 11.
14. Maitland, 1.
15. William McElwee, *History of England at a Glance* (English Universities Press, 1960), 32.
16. Christopher Hibbert, *The Story of England* (New York: Phaidon Press, 1992), 34.
17. *The Oxford Illustrated History of Britain,* ed. K. Morgan (New York: Oxford University Press, 1984), 81.
18. R. J. White, *A Short History of England* (Cambridge: Cambridge University Press, 1967), 35–36.
19. Cantor, 76.
20. Maitland, 2–3.
21. Cantor, 63–64.
22. Pollock and Maitland, 45.
23. Cantor, 81ff.
24. *Oxford Illustrated History of Britain,* 97.
25. McElwee, 51.
26. Cantor, 85.
27. Quoted in McElwee, 55.
28. *Oxford Illustrated History of England,* 103.
29. McElwee, 55.

CHAPTER 9: ENGLISH LAW FROM THE CONQUEST TO MAGNA CARTA, 1066–1215

1 Maitland, 6–7.
2 Quoted in Hibbert, *The Story of England*, 44.
3 Pollock and Maitland, 64–65. Notice the names Edmund and Edgar in this list and recall the cast of characters of Shakespeare's *King Lear*—a play set in the mystic world of early Britain.
4 Maitland, 7.
5 Pollock and Maitland, 77.
6 Maitland, 8.
7 Pollock and Maitland, 79.
8 Goldwin Albert Smith, *A History of England*, 4th ed. (New York: Scribner's, 1974), 34–35.
9 Cantor, 109.
10 Pollock and Maitland say simply of William Rufus that "whatever promises he made, he broke."
11 Cantor, 98.
12 Ibid., 96–97.
13 Cantor, 96
14 Maitland, 13.
15 Smith, 51–52.
16 Smith, 55.
17 Maitland, 122–3. A number of neighbors were thus placed upon oath and commanded to answer certain questions truthfully. One can see this inquest procedure as a direct ancestor of the modern jury when one recalls that the word *jury* comes from the Latin *iurare*, "to swear."
18 Ibid.,112.
19 Cantor, 56.
20 Ibid., 56–57.
21 Maitland, 125–6.
22 Ibid., 13.
23 Pollock and Maitland, 63.
24 Cantor, 71–73.
25 Pollock and Maitland, 167.
26 Hibbert, *The Story of England*, 62–63.
27 Ibid.
28 Strong, 69.

CHAPTER 10: FROM MAGNA CARTA TO THE ORIGINS OF PARLIAMENT

1. F. E. Halliday, *England: A Concise History* (London: Thames and Hudson, 1995), 49–51.
2. Halliday, 51.
3. Maitland, 15; Maitland and Pollock, 1:173.
4. J. C. Holt, *Magna Carta* (Cambridge: Cambridge University Press, 1992), 2. Magna Carta is as important to English law as it is to American. Maitland calls Magna Carta "the beginning of English statute law." According to Holt, "no other English legal enactment has enjoyed such long life."
5. Hibbert, 72.
6. Holt, 9–10.
7. Ibid., 17.
8. Ibid., 19.
9. Pollock and Maitland, 209.
10. Ibid., 182.
11. Maitland, 100.
12. Ibid.,100–101.
13. Smith, 114.
14. White, 82.
15. Maitland, 67.
16. White, 82–83.
17. White, 83.
18. Maitland, 19.
19. Smith, 114–15.
20. Maitland, 74–75.
21. White, 83–84.
22. Smith, 109.
23. Maitland, 19.
24. Burnham, 49–50.
25. Maitland, 114.
26. Halliday, 57.

CHAPTER 11: HENRY VII AND THE FOUNDATIONS OF TUDOR CONSTITUTIONALISM

1. G. R. Elton, *England under the Tudors* (London: Metheun), 1.
2. S. T. Bindoff, *Tudor England* (New York: Penguin Books), 1.
3. Elton, 2.
4. Elton, 6; Goldwin Smith, 191.
5. Bindoff, 7–8.
6. Elton, 16–17.
7. Ibid., 42–43.

8.   Smith, 192.
9.   Elton, 11 and 43.
10. Elton, 11.
11. For a review of the creation of Washington's cabinet, see for example, Richard Randall, *American Constitutional Development*, 1:65–66.
12. Bindoff, 59.
13. Ibid.
14. Elton, 12–13.
15. Bindoff, 59–60.
16. Maitland, 200 and 202.
17. Bindoff, 60–61.
18. Elton, 62.
19. Ibid., 46.
20. Ibid., 63.
21. Maitland, 221–4.
22. Ibid., 225–6.
23. The Seventh Amendment and the right of trial by jury does not apply to equity proceedings even today.
24. Maitland, 219.
25. Elton, 64.
26. Smith, 193.
27. Ibid., 194.
28. Elton, 57–59.
29. Maitland, 206–7.
30. Bindoff, 37.
31. Ibid., 175.
32. Ibid.
33. Ibid., 183.
34. Bindoff, 63.
35. Ibid., 65.
36. White, 108.

CHAPTER 12: HENRY VIII, THOMAS CROMWELL, AND THE TUDOR CONSTITUTIONAL REVOLUTION

1.   White, 112–13.
2.   Bindoff, 66–67.
3.   McElwee, 87.
4.   Ibid., 85.
5.   White, 112–13.
6.   Elton, 76–82.
7.   Bindoff, 75.

8. See Elton, 77: "Wolsey and not Henry was the effective ruler of the country."
9. Bindoff, 69.
10. McElwee, 89.
11. Elton, 102.
12. Bindoff, 79.
13. White, 114.
14. Elton, 106.
15. White, 113.
16. Elton, 109.
17. Ibid., 123.
18. Elton, 115.
19. Quoted in Richard O'Sullivan, "The Natural Law and the Common Law," in *Natural Law Institute Proceedings* 9 (Edward F. Barrett, ed., 1950), 31–33.
20. Elton, 127.
21. Ibid., 129.
22. Paolucci, *Brief History*, 23.
23. White, 115.
24. Quoted in Elton, 160.
25. McElwee, 90.
26. Ibid., 91.
27. Elton, 161–62.
28. Elton, 160–62.
29. Ibid., 166
30. Ibid., 167.
31. Paolucci, *Brief History*, 23.
32. White, 105–107.
33. McElwee, 101–102.
34. Ibid., 102.
35. White, 107.
36. Ibid., 108.

CHAPTER 13: JAMES I AND THE START OF THE ENGLISH CONSTITUTIONAL CRISIS OF THE SEVENTEENTH CENTURY

1. J. P. Kenyon, *Stuart England* (Gretna, LA: Pelican Books), 7–8.
2. Ibid., 35 and 41.
3. Ibid., 32.
4. Maitland, 250.
5. Kenyon (p. 33) mentions Wallace Notestein's "famous paper" of this title but calls it "deceptive (if not entirely false)."
6. Kenyon, 48.
7. Roy Strong, *The Story of Britain: A People's History* (London: Pimlico, 1998), 220.

8. Kenyon, 50.
9. James I, "Speech to Parliament" (March 21, 1610) in *The Stuart Constitution*, ed. J. P. Kenyon, 12–14.
10. The ceiling of the Banqueting Hall, the only remaining building in the royal Whitehall Palace, is so decorated.
11. Kenyon, 50.
12. Smith, 284.
13. Kenyon, 56.
14. Smith, 284.
15. Ibid., 291.
16. Maitland, 243. See also Strong, 228.
17. Douglas Kmiec, Stephen Presser, John Eastman, Raymond Marcin, *The History, Philosophy, and Structure of the American Constitution*, 2nd ed. (Newark, NJ: LexisNexis, 2004), 33–34.
18. Maitland, 270.
19. Smith, 295–6.
20. Maitland, 270–1.
21. Smith, 295.
22. Kenyon, 46. See Halliday, *England: A Concise History*, 108–9. In time, the term *Puritan* came to refer to anyone who "opposed the government for constitutional or religious reasons."
23. Halliday, 112. See also Kmiec and Presser, 41.
24. Kmiec and Presser, 42.
25. Strong, 229.
26. Maitland, 275.

CHAPTER 14: FROM CIVIL WAR TO GLORIOUS REVOLUTION

1. Strong, 230.
2. Smith, 308.
3. Maitland, 271.
4. Smith, 308.
5. J. G. Randall, *Constitutional Problems under Lincoln*, rev. ed. (Gloucester, MA: Peter Smith, 1963), 161–62.
6. Maitland, 273.
7. Smith, 309.
8. Ibid., 314–16.
9. Ibid., 309–10.
10. Ibid., 312.
11. Strong, 233.
12. Kmiec and Presser, 55.
13. Strong, 257, 260.

14. Ibid., 259.
15. Smith, 333–34; see also Strong, 259.
16. See *The Levellers in the English Revolution*, ed. G. E. Aylmer (Ithaca, NY: Cornell University Press, 1975) and Smith, 334–35.
17. Smith 337.
18. Quoted in Kmiec and Presser, 56–57.
19. "A Perfect Narrative of the Whole Proceedings of the High Court of Justice," in the *Trial of the King, in Westminster Hall, January 20–27, 1649*, licensed by Gilbert Mabbot, 4 How. S.T. 993 (1816), as quoted in Kmiec and Presser, 45.
20. Strong, 263.
21. Ibid., 281.
22. The initials of the five ministers closest to Charles after the fall of Clarendon spell out the word *CABAL*. See Smith, 359.
23. Strong, 289–90.
24. Goldwin Smith, 365.

CHAPTER 15: FROM CLASSICAL AND COMMON LAW BACKGROUND TO AMERICAN CONSTITUTIONALISM

1. Edward S. Corwin, *The Higher Law Background of American Constitutional Law* (Ithaca, NY: Cornell University Press, 1928/1955), 2.
2. Akhil Reed Amar, *America's Constitution: A Biography* (New York: Random House, 2006), 10.
3. Corwin, 4–5.
4. Kmiec and Presser, 1.
5. James Madison, letter to Thomas Jefferson, February 8, 1825, in *The Writings of James Madison*, vol. 9, ed. by Gaillard Hunt (1910), 218–21.
6. Declaration of Independence, 2nd para.
7. Corwin, 5–7.
8. Ibid., 6.
9. Jean-Jacques Rousseau, *On the Social Contract*, bk. 2, ch. 2, "That Sovereignty Is Indivisible."
10. Thomas Paine, *Political Writings (1837)*, 45–46.
11. Cicero, *De Legibus*, bk. 1, quoted in Corwin, 1–12.
12. Corwin, 17.
13. Quoted in Corwin, 24.
14. Stoner, 11.
15. Corwin, 26.
16. Roscoe Pound, *Interpretations of Legal History* (1923), 118. See also Corwin, 26.
17. John V. Orth, *Due Process of Law: A Brief History*, 6.
18. Fortescue, *De Laudibus Legum Angliae*, as cited in Corwin.
19. Corwin, 44–57.

20. Ibid.
21. See J. R. Pole, *Political Representation in England and the Origins of the American Republic* (New York: Macmillan/St. Martin's, 1966), 17. See also Carl Becker, *The Declaration of Independence*, ch. 2.
22. Corwin, 65.
23. John Locke, *Second Treatise of Government*, ed. Richard Cox (Arlington Heights: Harlan Davidson, 1982), ch. 11.
24. Corwin, 77.
25. See Duncan Kennedy, "The Structure of Blackstone's Commentaries," in *Buffalo Law Review* 28: 205–382, and Daniel Boorstin, *The Mysterious Science of the Law: An Essay on Blackstone's Commentaries* (Cambridge, MA: Harvard University Press, 1941).
26. Quoted in Douglas Kmiec, Stephen Presser, John Eastman, and Raymond Marcin, *Individual Rights and the American Constitution*, 2nd ed. (Newark, NJ: LexisNexis, 2004), 6.
27. Ibid.

CONCLUSION

1. Lord Bolingbroke, "A Dissertation Upon Parties," in *The Works of Lord Bolingbroke*, 2:88, quoted in Charles Howard McIlwain, *Constitutionalism: Ancient and Modern* (Ithaca, NY: Cornell University Press), 3.
2. McIlwain, 14.

Index